How to Run a Dog Business

Putting Your Career Where Your Heart Is
2nd Edition

Veronica Boutelle

Dogwise™
Publishing

Wenatchee, Washington U.S.A.

How to Run a Dog Business
Putting Your Career Where Your Heart Is, 2nd Edition
Veronica Boutelle

Dogwise Publishing
A Division of Direct Book Service, Inc.
403 South Mission Street, Wenatchee, Washington 98801
1-509-663-9115, 1-800-776-2665
www.dogwisepublishing.com / info@dogwisepublishing.com

Cover Design: Dan Phairas, Bangarang Media www.bangarangmedia.com
Interior Design: Lindsay Peternell

Library of Congress Cataloging-in-Publication Data
Boutelle, Veronica, author.
  How to run a dog business : putting your career where your heart is / Veronica Boutelle. -- 2nd edition.
     pages cm
  Includes index.
  ISBN 978-1-61781-136-4
  1. Dogs--Training--Vocational guidance. 2. Dog trainers. 3. Small business--Management. 4. New business enterprises--Management. I. Title.
  SF431.B68 2013
  636.7'0887--dc23

                            2013043245

ISBN: 978-1-61781-136-4

Printed in the U.S.A.

Dedication

I dedicate this book to my clients. Your courageous decision to pursue your dream of working with dogs for a living is why I do what I do.

Acknowledgements

Thank you first to my editor, Rikke Jorgensen, for your tremendous improvements to this work, your straightforward advice, and your invaluable support. Thank you to my dog*tec partner in crime Gina Phairas for too much to mention here. Thank you to our amazing manager and director of ops and all things, Deborsha, for keeping us all afloat. And thank you to all the clients I've had the pleasure to work with and learn from over the first ten years of our dog*tec adventure.

On a personal note, I thank my husband Patrick for making sure I remember to eat—and that there is something to eat—when I'm writing. And I thank my dad Ken for supporting everything I've ever chosen to do.

Table of Contents

Foreword

Helping the Helper

As Director of the San Francisco SPCA Academy for Dog Trainers, I had the opportunity to see Veronica in action when she ran the behavior and training department at the SF-SPCA. She said that what she most liked about the dog training world was helping other trainers to do their jobs. She mused about doing exactly that full-time, and the result was dog*tec, her consulting and seminar business, and now this book, *How to Run a Dog Business*. Veronica loves and respects dog trainers and genuinely loves helping them. And, aside from the invaluable practicalities, counsel, structure, and support she provides, there is her real-time model of how to handle clients, in this case the client being the trainer: authentically, with respect, patience and empathy. Not to mention the model of finding the niche that you like and are good at. A common theme of hers is playing to strengths and using solid strategies to handle everything else.

There was a Monday some months ago when I awoke to 86 emails in my inbox, all but five of which fell into two categories: junk and "HELP!" The triage strategy I used to sort through the mayhem was pure Veronica. The fact that I had a triage strategy and that turning to it came immediately, without agony, was pure Veronica. I could almost hear her voice in my head: "Well, of course you can't do all of them. So let's talk about how much time on a typical day you want to put into answering cold, pro-bono, distance consult requests." (They have a category!) "Once we have that time, we can work backwards and prioritize. Then we'll think about how, on a particularly bad day, you'll raise the bar and end up deleting or referring more." A plan. A conscious plan. No, wait, better—a system. First delete the junk, then delete or refer requests from people you don't know, leaving colleagues and former students. Then the bad day clause kicks in, so delete or refer anything less concise than a few lines, leaving a manageable handful. Divide these into the time available and, voila, a time allocation for each. Reply and then get on with the rest of the bad—time-wise bad—day. With some actual energy.

I also often get flashes of Veronica when I am in the offices of mental health professionals (which I have been known to be seen in). Two instances spring to mind. In one, a psychologist sagely and simply observed that I had difficulty setting limits. There are options in the face of such observations. There's the Teflon option, such as the dismissive "duh" or the "that's just who I am" or, Teflon with a side of solipsism, "somebody has to...(save the world, the world being, of course, the dogs, all of them)." There's the externalizing option, inevitably some variation on "how do I get them to stop...(inviting me, and only me apparently, to save the world, i.e., all the dogs)." The best option is, of course, the Veronica Option: absorption and reflection. "Let's think about this," she'd say and then help you think about it, always in a useful, non-stewy way. Everyone should be so lucky as to have a Veronica Option when these mental forks in the road appear. I hope that readers of this book will choose absorb-reflect a lot. Several times per page actually. If you do this, you'll end up with a tidy stable of Veronica Options.

The second Veronica flash came about when my curiosity got the better of me and I one day asked a psychiatrist who seemed to genuinely enjoy and be engaged by what she was doing, how she could stand to be a repository for people's angst and suffering all day long. She paused only briefly before saying, "I like my patients." It probably shouldn't have, but it blindsided me. The same theme has been oft-mused by my friend and colleague, Janis Bradley, whose bare reply to students and fellow trainers, when they lament the difficulties inherent in counseling dog guardians is: "you gotta find a way to like your clients." The clients being the humans, not the dogs. As Veronica so aptly points out in the book you're about to read, dog training pulls people who have great, great affinity for dogs. By happenstance, some may also have a liking of, gift for, or training in helping people. But too often, in the dog trainer's drama, the client is the perpetrator, the dog the victim and the dog trainer the tormented superhero. Burn-out city, that plot is.

In helping professions, wherein this role is more frankly acknowledged than in dog training, helping the helper is a long-standing theme. Support and replenishment for those who deal with humans in need is also a hot topic in domestic situations—caring for elderly or ill parents, nurturing a special needs child, sticking by a spouse through thick and thin. It is gratifying indeed to see the complexity and helping aspects of dog training acknowledged, taken apart, and made manageable. It will pull good people into the field and retain many more who might have otherwise burned out. I can honestly think of no better way to save all the dogs.

Jean Donaldson, author of *Culture Clash, Fight!, Mine!,* and *Dogs Are From Neptune*

August, 2007

Introduction

Why a second edition?

In a moment I'm going to ask you to consider the characteristics of successful business owners. One of them is a commitment to constantly learning, to never assuming you know all there is to know about what you do—about dogs, dog behavior, and about running your business. At dog*tec we've always strived to practice what we preach, which means we're always learning, too. As I write this updated introduction, we've just celebrated our tenth anniversary of helping dog professionals succeed in their businesses. As you can imagine, I've learned a new thing or two since I wrote the first edition of this book six years ago. My goal with the second edition has been to incorporate our ten years of experience helping dog business owners make their living doing what they love.

This edition includes an expanded marketing chapter, along with a brand new one dedicated just to online marketing. Another new chapter covers building the perfect staff to help your business move forward while lightening your own workload. And you'll find additional advice on packaging your services, setting your policies, and avoiding dog pro burnout, along with an updated and expanded resources section. Speaking for myself and the entire dog*tec team, we hope you find this book a helpful and encouraging voice at your shoulder as you pursue the work of starting or growing your dog business.

Is owning a dog business right for you?

Some dream of it from childhood—working with dogs for a living. I remember gathering all my stuffed dogs onto a large blanket and pretending to go down a river on our "raft," encountering all manner of adventures along the way. Or piling the plush pooches into my wagon to walk down the street for the mail, stopping now and then for a quick training lesson. If someone had asked me at five years of age what I wanted to be when I grew up, I'd have said I wanted to be an animal teacher. As it turned out, I became a teacher, but of humans. It wasn't until I began to cast around for a second career that I stumbled into dog training.

Most dog trainers, walkers, sitters, daycare and boarding facility operators, and other dog pros come to the profession as a second career. Nearly everyone engaged in a dog business has a deep love of animals, and when this combines with a high degree of frustration with (or aversion to!) traditional jobs, the lure of working with dogs full time becomes strong. Unfortunately for those who wish to work with dogs the choices are slim. There are few jobs available and most rarely pay much above minimum wage. Almost never do they come with health or other benefits. So for all but a few of us, to earn a living as a provider of professional dog services means starting our own businesses.

The six characteristics of successful dog business owners

But before you start your business or dive deeper into financial and legal commitments with an existing one, take a few moments to consider whether you are truly heading in a direction that is right for you.

It's easy to glamorize the benefits of being one's own boss—the flexible scheduling, being able to do things the way you see fit, being in control of your own destiny. When a business is running well, all of this is true. But the downsides are equally important—there's no one to write your monthly paycheck, no set hours and accountability to make sure the unexciting but necessary administrative tasks are completed, and the business's success or failure rests on your shoulders. Many people find working for themselves more of a challenge than anticipated, and it seems that some personalities are better suited to the life of a small business owner than others.

Here are six qualities we've found help dog pros succeed. Do you have these? Are you willing to cultivate the ones you don't?

Confidence

Easier said than done, right? Over the years we've had the privilege of helping many dog professionals build and manage their small businesses, and our conversations reveal that moments of great uncertainty and insecurity come with the territory. You may worry, for example, that you'll be "found out" as somehow less accomplished or skilled than you're perceived to be. But dwelling there won't get you very far. It's hard enough when family, friends, or partners cast doubt on your business plans, so don't give in to personal pessimism.

We're not advising cockiness, which implies a closed-off attitude. Confident business owners listen to criticism, but gauge it against their own inner values and vision, accepting what fits and rejecting what doesn't. It may help here to practice the motto, "Fake it 'til you make it." Confidence may not be innate, but it can be gained.

Risk taking

Think of the times in your life when you grew the most. Chances are they corresponded to moments of great personal challenge. Growth rarely happens when we're comfortable. Many new business owners have to dip into their savings or borrow money—what if you have to? Does the mere thought give you the heebie-jeebies? Starting a dog training business takes less capital than most enterprises, but you still run the risk of losing money and possibly failing. It takes tenacity and perspective to face such prospects and still work hard and enthusiastically. I've seen many dog pros quit or go back to part-time work long before their businesses could reasonably be expected to succeed.

You may not think of yourself as a risk-taker, but by thinking about or starting your own business you've already shown you have that potential, leaving behind a steady income and risking money, time, and energy in the pursuit of more meaningful and satisfying work.

Harness that potential and keep looking for ways to dream bigger and embrace uncertainty. Not all of your ideas will work, but that's why they're called risks. Again, a little imagination here can help. Act as if you're a risk-taker, and you may soon find you have a taste for it. The following four attributes can also help.

Problem solving

There's no getting around it. Even with the above qualities driving you and your business, you'll experience failure. Some risks don't pan out, confidence can't always correct a financial emergency, and you may find yourself ambling down the wrong path. So now what?

Interview any successful business owner and, if she's honest, she'll tell you that before every success came a few failures—the marketing plan that didn't pay off, the day care attendant who didn't work out, the class she couldn't fill. Failures sting, but with a brave curiosity, you can choose to see them as opportunities. Each failure gives you valuable data about what doesn't work or what your clients don't want. Use this data to plot your new path.

You will face challenges and problems throughout your business career. While you don't have to enjoy solving problems, you do need a willingness to tackle them head on and not sweep them under the rug.

Creative thinking

Nicolaus Copernicus and Galileo Galilei, working against strong established opposition, argued that the Earth revolves around the sun, despite what our own eyes would have us believe. History-makers challenge convention. Looking closer to home, where would our understanding of puppy socialization be without Ian Dunbar? You don't have to change the laws of science or the prevailing methods of modern dog training to be a successful business owner, but don't be afraid to challenge convention.

It's tempting to use another dog pro's business model as a blueprint, especially when starting out, but it may not be the most logical, efficient or effective. Dog trainers are quick to question their peers' training methods and strategies. We'd do well to bring the same discerning eye to common business practices in our industry, too, as many of them do not serve us well. For example, unless you're turning clients away, a 24-hour cancellation policy may not be doing you any favors. Every other local dog pro may use this policy, but if it's not doing what it's supposed to do—save you money by guarding against empty appointment slots—then you need a creative change.

Or consider the coaching model—teaching clients how to train their own dogs. This has been the standard training model for decades, but it frequently results in client failure and frustration, and low incomes and burnout for trainers. More and more trainers are turning to approaches like day training, taking over the training themselves and transferring the results to the client. This change required creative thinking, and a willingness to challenge convention.

The point is, avoid the temptation to copy your colleagues and competitors, instead cultivating your own independent, creative business thinking based on client needs and backed by collecting data on what is and isn't working.

Sitzfleisch

This German word sounds like what it means, combining "sit" and "flesh" to describe the quality of perseverance—of keeping your seat at your desk, so to speak. Starting and managing a small business requires patience and endurance, often more than we initially expect. Bestselling author Malcolm Gladwell points out that no matter what the profession—composer, ice skater, basketball player—true mastery requires 10,000 hours of practice. That works out to 20 hours a week for ten years! Think back to the first dog you walked, the first one you trained. How many hours did it take (how many clickers clicked?) before you began to feel even slightly competent?

Bring that same persistence to your business. The success of a marketing plan, for example, is better measured in months and years than in hours or days. Invest, endure, persist. Who knows what you'll give up if you give up too soon? You'll likely find a particular need for self-discipline when it comes to those parts of the business above and beyond dealing with dogs such as marketing, bookkeeping, and following up with clients.

Willingness to keep learning

Successful business people are honest about what they don't know, and rather than let it discourage them, they work hard at continuing education and professional development. They also weigh the time and energy a new skill demands against their own talents and resources, and determine when hiring outside help (an accountant or bookkeeper, for example) makes more sense.

I assume you already take your continuing education in animal behavior seriously, and I'm probably preaching to the choir given that you're holding this book, but you must make equal time for learning how to run your small business. Read books and articles and attend workshops and web seminars. Consider hiring a business coach to help bolster areas you're struggling with. Recognize that your business skills—customer service, marketing, service development, systems development, hiring, training, and managing staff, etc.—are every bit as critical to your success as your ability to train, walk, or care for dogs.

Practice makes perfect

As you think about and work on these six characteristics, you'll no doubt find them complementary. Like the complicated interplay of hand muscles, developing one will involve and strengthen the others. Problem solving calls upon persistence, and risk-taking involves creative thinking. Like your first days working with dogs, you may feel a little clumsy at first. But with time and patience your skills will improve—we've seen it time and again in our work with dog pros.

Again, think back on your first days working with dogs. The first time you tried to walk more than two at a time. Your first day juggling leash, clicker, and treat bag. The first nervous dog who needed a pill twice a day. The first dog you groomed, the first nails you clipped. Chances are your dexterity had room for improvement. But you gave it time and practice and your skills grew.

Business skills work much the same way, and keep in mind that even the most successful dog business owners endured clumsy early days and moments of doubt.

Who is this book for?

If you're already in business for yourself, you've probably experienced some of the common frustrations and pitfalls. There's the obvious dismay of not having enough clients or being able to make ends meet. And the surprise of one day waking up to realize that your business is running you, rather than the other way around. This common phenomenon can sneak up on you easily, a combination of early systems failing under the weight of increased business, of initial decisions that made perfect sense at the beginning coming back to haunt you as the business grew, and the press of day to day activities robbing your attention from the big picture needs of your enterprise. If you're already knee deep in these stressors, this book can help you dig out, create a fresh start, and get business booming. And if you're just getting started, the aim is to help you start off in control and stay there as you achieve success.

A word on the businesses covered in this book

Though groomers, veterinary clinics, and other pet care providers are likely to find many of the basic concepts and ideas in this book useful, and while some of the advice given in these pages is true for any business, the book is intentionally and specifically designed for the needs, challenges, and success of dog trainers, dog walkers, pet sitters, and daycare and boarding operators.

Reality check—do you really get paid to play with dogs all day?

Unfortunately not. Hands-on dog time varies by profession and business type, but all dog businesses entail more than working with dogs. As you'll see, a large portion of your time will be spent marketing your business (which isn't as frightening or awful as it sounds). Then there's the administrative time spent answering and returning phone calls and emails, handling client paperwork, and taking care of general tasks like bookkeeping. And don't underestimate the driving. Most sitters, walkers, and trainers spend a good deal of time in their cars. Another consideration for trainers is the realization early on that in most cases training owners, not dogs, is the primary task.

These are all important facts to face as you decide if a career as a dog pro is right for you. Even so, life with the dogs is a hard living to beat. If you agree, this book is for you.

1

New Pups: Getting

Started

Before committing money and time to a new career—and before you leave your day job—I suggest you find ways to experience your chosen field firsthand to make sure it is right for you. Many dog lovers attend a dog training program or start a business only to find they don't enjoy the day-to-day routines of the job, despite an enduring love of dogs.

Volunteer

If you haven't spent a lot of time with different types of dogs or dogs in groups, try volunteering at places where dogs congregate, such as a local shelter or daycare. Some people are surprised to find that they don't enjoy the company of all dogs nearly as much as they do their family pooch.

Volunteering with a dog pro is another excellent way to get an insider's view of the career you are considering. If you are interested in training, offer to assist in a local trainer's classes. Would-be dog walkers can try to find a local walker who might welcome your company on a walk or two. Thinking of pet sitting or boarding? Ask a professional sitter if you can ride along, or a facility operator if you can help out.

Be careful to choose someone who is reputable and has credentials and experience. Then let them know you are interested in the profession and would like to offer your assistance in return for some experience. Buy them lunch or coffee to talk it over if they have time. If you are professional in your manner and sincere in your attitude (and gratitude) they'll likely be glad for the help.

Go to school

Going to school is a relatively recent option for would-be dog trainers, but already there are a profusion of dog training programs to choose from. Although you can still legally declare yourself a dog trainer without any formal education, this is becoming less acceptable as the industry professionalizes. Consider this to your advantage—you will be much more successful and help more people and dogs if you learn the trade. And, though you may have grown up with and loved dogs all your life, don't cheat yourself by falling into the "I'm really good with dogs" trap. There is a high degree of skill and knowledge involved in training, and it is too fascinating to miss out on—the study of canine body language, how dogs think and learn, the science behind behavior modification, the effects of nature and nurture on behavior—and the list goes on and on. Yes, there is a certain amount of just "being good with dogs" involved with being a good trainer. And yes, there is craft to dog training. But the craft without the science is limited and often leads to misinterpretations of dog behavior, which leads to training choices that can be inefficient and even dangerous.

Traditionally, dog trainers have been self taught, but this is changing rapidly. Dr. Ian Dunbar founded the Association of Professional Dog Trainers (APDT) in 1993 hoping to bring quality education and scientific standards to a profession that had long relied solely on mentorship, apprenticeship, or simply "being good with dogs." The impact of the APDT has been profound, particularly in the area of trainer certification. Schools for dog trainers have sprouted all over the country, science-based training has revolutionized the field, and clients are increasingly demanding to work with trainers who have formal education and training. An unfortunate side effect of this overwhelmingly positive development is the inception of many less-than-reputable programs for dog trainers, some of which do more harm than good by spreading old misconceptions and harmful practices, others that simply take your money and teach you very little. But we also see dog training slowly becoming recognized as a skilled profession and a number of strong programs gaining ground and educating greater numbers of trainers. Dog trainers who graduate from such places are changing dog training from an anecdotally-based approach to a science-based approach, and the profession, dog owners, and dogs are all the better for it.

Being well trained, so to speak, can only be to your benefit, and what's more, it is the professionally responsible thing to do, and reduces your liability risk. If you decide to commit to the concept of education, and I strongly recommend that you do, the next step is to find the right program for you, and here, you cannot be too thorough or discriminating. There are many schools out there, but as I've mentioned, they vary greatly in content, approach to training, and quality. As you search for schools, keep these considerations in mind:

- Who are the instructors? What are their qualifications?

- What approach are they taking to dog training? Are their methods scientifically sound and humane? Are they in keeping with recent research?

- You'll see a lot of buzzwords. Some you want to see include: positive reinforcement, operant and classical conditioning, scientific method. Some to be wary of include: leadership, dominance, eclectic, balanced, and inclusive. Also, avoid anyone who promises immediate and dramatic results.

- To be ready to take clients, you need a good balance of theory and practice. Online or other remote courses can be fantastic additions to a direct education, but cannot serve as a replacement for a hands-on program and experience.

Education and training programs for walkers and sitters are definitely scarcer. There is only one training and certification program for dog walkers, the dog*tec Dog Walking Academy. Given that it would be inappropriate to toot that horn too much here, I'll just say that there's further information at the back of the book should you be interested in learning more. Pet sitters can join the Association of Pet Sitting Excellence (APSE), National Association of Professional Pet Sitters (NAPPS), and/or Pet Sitters International (PSI) and attend their yearly conferences.

I strongly recommend that daycare owners have as much dog training education as possible—it will greatly increase your enjoyment of the work and the safety of yourself, others, and the dogs. See the Resources section at the back of this book (hereafter referred to as Resources) for a list of daycare programs as well as respected dog training schools, and books pertaining to daycare and training.

Read

While not a substitute for hands-on experience, reading is key to mastering the theory behind training, and it will make you a better trainer, walker, sitter, or daycare or boarding operator. Similar to schools, all books and authors are not the same, so use the guidelines for finding a training program to help you build your library. For a list of must-reads, and how to get them, see the Resources at the back of this book.

Finding an older dog: how to find and keep a mentor

Connecting with a strong, knowledgeable mentor can make a great difference at the beginning and throughout your career. You want someone who is good at what they do, and adept at talking about it; someone who is willing to take the time to work with you and answer your questions because they care about the profession and recognize that being a mentor pushes them further, too. In short, you want a good teacher, confidant, and colleague.

To find your mentor, make a list of the various people in your area who offer the services you want to learn. Contact each person and introduce yourself. Tell them you're interested in entering the profession and ask if they would be willing to chat with you for a few moments. If you enjoy the conversation, offer to take them to lunch to continue it. Such conversations give you a chance to make a connection and build an early sense of the person's approach and professionalism. If things are going well, offer to assist them. From there you can begin to build a mentoring relationship.

For a mentor-protégé relationship to work in the long term it is important that the mentor benefits, too. Don't be afraid to ask what you can do to help your mentor, but also take initiative where appropriate. You'll have a lot of questions—be mindful of when you ask them (i.e., not during consults and training sessions), and how many you fire off in a single sitting. A good mentor will spend time on your education, but don't ask for too much. Try keeping a small notebook to jot down your questions, and then prioritize so that you get the most pressing ones answered. Suggest arranging a specific time for your questions, such as after a class for trainers or during car rides for walkers and sitters.

Schools and seminars: the importance of continuing education

Your education shouldn't end after you become certified. By the time you are certified you will have realized how much there still is to know, and ongoing research and the constant refinement of methods make continuing education exciting and necessary for staying up to date.

Seminars are a great way to keep up on your education, and to meet and network with colleagues. As not all seminars and speakers share the same quality, choose with care how you spend your time and money. Once there try not to be charmed by the speaker. Instead, ask hard questions. What evidence do they have for their assertions? How does what they're saying compare with what you've read and learned previously? What is the scientific basis for their concepts?

You can find seminars and educational conferences by joining local mailing groups and keeping an eye on the CCPDT, APDT, IAABC, Dog Seminars Directory, and other professional websites. There are also quickly expanding web seminar opportunities, allowing you to keep up to date from the comfort and convenience of home. See the Resources at the end of the book for additional information.

Keep learning in between seminars. Dogwise is a fantastic source of dog-related books and videos. Join their mailing list and they'll keep you up to date on all the new titles. And Tawzer Dog Videos specializes in taping seminars across the country and making them available to folks not lucky enough to be there in person. These resources are available at the back of the book.

2

Finances and Systems for Your Business

A question I'm frequently asked, and with good reason, is whether or not you can actually make a living working with dogs. The short answer is yes. But most people want to know whether their business idea will work, and we always start any one-on-one business coaching by crunching numbers to assess risk versus potential success. To set people up for organizational as well as financial success, I also recommend spending some time considering the systems involved in the day-to-day running of a business.

Crunching the numbers

The concept of budgeting is not a thrilling one, but it doesn't need to be overwhelming. To be sure you'll have money for the electricity bills, begin with this simple assessment: figure out how much you need to live on each year. Be detailed and realistic and don't forget the annual or occasional expenses like taxes, insurance, car repairs, etc. Then assess your competition—what are others in the area charging, and what services do they provide? An Internet search backed by phone calls to others in your area (you can ask a friend to call for you if you feel uncomfortable) will give you plenty to go on. Use this information to determine a range of possible rates—a low, a high, an average. Now estimate a reasonable, conservative number of clients per month and year, being careful to consider seasonal variables. Then do the math—does it add up?

If the numbers don't look initially promising, don't give up—go back to the drawing board to see what kind of creative solutions are waiting. You might add another service to increase revenue, such as adding walking services to a training or sitting business. Bringing in an independent contractor or employee (see Chapter 8 for guidelines) can increase volume and thus income. Or think about a new approach to services already available in your area. For example, if other trainers are seeing clients once a week in their homes and teaching them to work their own dogs, you may be able to charge more for the convenience and efficiency of owner absent day training (but be sure to teach the owners what they need to know to keep the training intact).

Start-up capital is another consideration. Little is needed for most dog pro businesses. Trainers usually work from a home office. In this case, the main expenses will be start-up support and marketing which, as you'll see in Chapter 4, do not need to be excessive. For a training business you might plan for somewhere in the neighborhood of $1,500 to $6,000 for an average low-budget start up, not including education costs. Walkers and sitters, you have the same expenses plus investment in an appropriate vehicle if you don't already own one. Daycare and boarding operators and trainers wishing to open training facilities, you will experience much higher start-up costs, as you must factor in a building lease or purchase, any build-out construction costs, technology infrastructure, and materials. These expenses depend on too many variables—local real estate rates, the condition of your chosen space, your build-out vision, the complexity of your services, etc.—to provide an average cost range. But you can work with a commercial real estate agent, contractor, and business consultant to generate accurate numbers for your own situation.

See the Resources for a detailed chart comparing start-up and ongoing costs, as well as many additional factors. You will also find a basic budget outline and business plan information.

Create effective systems from the beginning

Though it may be tempting to start taking clients and see what happens, you're best served by setting up systems from the beginning for things like client intake, billing, client homework instructions, policies and procedures, etc. You will probably adjust them as you grow, but having systems to begin with will make things smoother as you take your first client calls and as business picks up. It will also increase your look of professionalism. See Chapter 7 for more details on policies and the Resources for help with paperwork.

To the extent possible, avoid making decisions that are "just for now." If you have a desire or intention to expand your business later—to open a facility or add a service you aren't yet ready to provide, for example—keep that in mind as you start your business. Don't make decisions you will have to undo later. Take your present and future into account when tackling things such as choosing a business name, working on your marketing, creating your systems, defining your geographic service area, and setting up your business legally. For example, you wouldn't want to call yourself "Cuddles Pet Sitting" if your goal is to eventually become a trainer and help people with aggression issues. And a system of keeping client contact information in physical folders will mean a lot of data entry later when you realize you need your contact information in a centralized location for ease of marketing. Or, before you take a dog walking or pet sitting client two towns away because you feel you should "take everything you can get at the beginning," stop to consider the stress of having to let those clients go later on, or the consequences of accidentally building a strong word of mouth business in the wrong place.

CASE STUDY

Adam was delighted with his dog walking business. He enjoyed a client wait list and had far exceeded his financial expectations. But he was exhausted. He and his employees were running up huge gas bills and everyone felt like the proverbial chicken without a head. The systems Adam used to screen and schedule clients, and his policy of allowing part-time clients, meant that every walker in his business walked slightly different packs each day and put in extra miles picking up dogs who lived across town from each other. This had all worked fine in the beginning, but now that his business was running at full capacity, the inefficiency was causing too much extra work. Adam put several changes into play. He reworked the packs to group dogs by geography (being careful to make sure they were temperamentally suited to each other, too!) and sent a letter to clients letting them know that beginning in the new year billing would be done at the beginning of each month to "reserve" their dog's full-time spot in the pack, even if they didn't go out every day. For clients who had been used to part time, he offered to help find alternatives if they chose not to move to full-time status. Adam was relieved to find that only a few decided to move on. Most understood the value of his service and were happy to commit, and the open spots were quickly filled from the wait list. By the end of January, Adam happily reported that he was working far fewer hours for the same income.

Get professional help with your business

Some dog pros are experienced business people who have chosen to open a dog business, but most have never run a business before and, as noted previously, it is often the only option available to make a living working with dogs. One secret to success in business is to do what you do well and get help with the rest. So if you're not a business person by trade or instinct, get some support to help ensure your success. Almost everyone will need the services of a good bookkeeper or accountant, an attorney, and an insurance agent as will be discussed in Chapter 3. Learn from colleagues, join professional organizations, and consider hiring a business coach. There are resources you can tap listed at the back of this book.

3

Legalities and Liability

Is there a pit in your stomach as you open this chapter? Be assured it'll be gone by the time you finish reading. Legalizing and protecting your business is so much easier—and comes at a far more reasonable price—than you might fear. A little time spent now will allow you to work with the dogs in the comfort and security that comes from knowing your paperwork is in order and your assets are protected from lawsuits.

Legal requirements
Business license
Your business license is a permit from your city to do business within their borders, and in most cities is easy and inexpensive to acquire. Expect to pay on average $40-$150 per year. Application forms are usually between one and three pages long with straightforward questions. If your city asks for your yearly revenue or similar numbers you're unsure of, just give your best guess.

To pursue your license, begin at your city's website. Search for "[Your City] home page" on any search engine and it will come up. Most city sites have downloadable business license application forms—some even let you apply online. Sometimes the downloadable forms come with instructions; sometimes the instructions are separate or exist only on the website. Wherever they are, read them thoroughly before filling out the application.

If you intend to run your business from home you may need a zoning exemption. Cities designate neighborhoods for particular uses. In an area zoned for residential use you may need to file zoning exemption paperwork with your business license. This is usually a simple form in which you show that you won't significantly impact your neighborhood by putting up signage or having clients coming and going at all hours, for example. If administrative work is all you'll be doing—the basic phone and computer tasks—you should receive the exemption easily. Often, it's anything but obvious from a city's website that a zoning exemption is required, so check carefully. Even if you find nothing on the site, it's worth calling their help number to make sure—filing the exemption paperwork is much less complicated if your business license application hasn't been turned down already for zoning reasons.

Do you have to have a business license? Technically, yes. What happens if you don't? In most cases, nothing. In the worst case, large fines. Cities generally don't go searching for businesses operating without licenses, and if they find out at all it will likely be due to a complaint filed about your business. But given that having a license is required by law and that it's simple to get (plan to spend an hour or two on the whole process) and usually costs little, it's certainly worth your while. What's more, it professionalizes and legitimizes your business and gives you one less thing to worry about.

Fictitious or assumed business name

The fictitious business name (FBN) sometimes goes by other monikers, such as an assumed business name (ABN) or a doing business as certificate (DBA). These are all the same thing. You don't need a fictitious business name if you are using your own name, e.g., Lisa Smith's Dog Training, to run your business. But if you plan to operate under a name other than your own, such as "Good Dog Training," you need to file this paperwork with your county clerk's office. As with the business license, the FBN application process is simple and inexpensive—usually around $40-$80 in total.

Registering a fictitious business name does two things. First, it announces to your community who is responsible for your business. This practice prevents people from setting up businesses to use for nefarious activities while hiding their actual identities. To accomplish the announcement part of your fictitious business name you are required to publish a short statement about the creation and ownership of your business for a certain number of weeks in a local paper. When you file for your FBN you'll receive information about this requirement. Generally, a local paper or two will contact you and offer to take care of this step for you. In most cases the $40-$80 for your FBN includes this cost, though you will pay the newspaper separately.

The second purpose of the FBN is to avoid a confusing duplication of business names in the community—two businesses in one county called Good Dog Training is impractical. Your FBN gives you the exclusive right in your county to use the business name you've chosen.

To apply for your FBN search the Internet for "[Your County] clerk's office." Once on the site, look for any reference to "business" or "fictitious business name" or "filings." Many county clerk sites allow you to search online to check that the business name you wish to register is available. If they don't, you may be able to call and ask them to do a search for you over the phone. In some cases you still need to go to your county clerk's office to do the search in person at a computer station or—gulp!—on microfiche. But this is rare. Once you've determined the name is available, you fill out the application—online if you can, or by downloading the form and mailing it in. In some places you have to apply in person, but this is unusual. Read the directions carefully—FBNs are often required to be submitted in multiple copies. But the paperwork itself is generally simple—rarely longer than two pages.

A quick note—if you are struggling with choosing a business name, see Chapter 4 for some help.

Service mark

While your fictitious business name protects your name in your own county, other dog professionals can use the same name elsewhere. If you wish to protect your name and/or logo further you can opt for a service mark, which is a trademark for a service oriented business. A service mark gives you exclusive rights to use a certain name and/or logo image to sell your services. A trademark would do the same thing for selling a physical product.

Service marks come in two sizes: the state level and the federal. Most state service mark applications require minimal paperwork (around two simple pages, submitted with a sample of your name and/or logo in use—such as on a business card). State service marks tend to be inexpensive, too. So if you are very fond of your chosen name and/or logo image and plan to spend time, energy, and considerable capital promoting your business, you might give some consideration to a state service mark. An application form and directions can be downloaded from your secretary of state website by searching for "[Your State] Secretary of State home page."

A federal service mark is a bit more complicated and costly. The current fee is $375 and the paperwork is too difficult to tackle without an attorney. All in, filing a national service mark can easily run you $1,500. Note that you must work across state lines in order to qualify for a federal mark. And while the federal mark holds more power than the state mark, it is unlikely a national company will come knocking on your door if you only operate regionally. Just don't name your business Petsmart!

In short, unless you are considering a national agenda that involves franchising, writing a book or widely syndicated column, going on the speaker circuit, etc., you probably don't need a national mark. But if you have plans for a future empire, a national service mark is essential. To check name availability, go to www.uspto.gov (the United States Patent and Trademark Office) to do an online search. You can also download an application form, but this is the one piece of paperwork I do recommend engaging an attorney for. See the Resources for an attorney with dog business experience.

URLs

Web addresses, or domain names, have to be purchased. Even if you apply for all the service marks and your FBN, someone else can still own the domain name you want. For this reason, it's advisable to search the Internet for your chosen name before you proceed further. Do the search even if you don't mean to set up a website at this time. You will almost certainly need a website, and without a doubt potential clients will look for you online. Don't let them find someone else! Purchasing a domain name is inexpensive and easy.

Keep in mind that you may not get your first choice—it's hard these days to come up with an original domain name no one else has thought of and bought up. If your first choice—say gooddog. com—isn't available, don't panic. Look at variations, sticking with a .com (rather than .net or .biz, etc.) if you possibly can. You might, for example, try a variation that includes your services or your geographical region, such as gooddogtraining.com or gooddogseattle. com.

One last tip: Once you've found a name you like and made sure it's available, purchase additional domains if you can. Most people use the .com address, but purchasing .info, .biz, .net, etc. as well is a low-cost way to reduce the chances that someone else will use your business name.

A Word on the Internet

If having a presence on the Internet is new to you, here is a quick primer: Your website is like a large, online brochure. It is your marketing vehicle. Your web address, or domain name, is where you park your vehicle—it's where your website lives on the Internet: www.yourbusinessnamehere.com. Your email address is how people reach you on the Internet. In this case: You@yourbusinessnamehere.com.

FEIN

The FEIN, or Federal Employer Identification Number (sometimes shortened to just EIN or referred to as your Tax ID Number), is like a social security number for your business. If you are going to have employees, you'll need one. You'll also need one if you decide to become a limited liability company (see below), even if you never plan to hire employees.

Remarkably, even though this little number comes from the IRS, it is free and easy to get. Simply go to www.irs.gov and do a search for form SS-4. It's a single straightforward page with a number to call to get help. Or you can call and get your EIN over the phone in about five minutes. (If only the IRS were always so helpful!) Find additional contact information in the Resources at the back of this book.

Liability issues

For anyone who is or is planning to be a dog professional, knowing the risks involved in your profession is essential, as are the steps you can take to professionalize and protect yourself.

How big is the risk?

Dog professions are often thought of as high risk because—simply put—dogs are animals and animals bite. But how great is the risk actually? Unfortunately there are no official legal statistics kept to help us answer this question. Anecdotally, in my thirteen years of experience working with dog pros across the country, first as Director of Behavior & Training for the San Francisco SPCA and then through dog*tec, I am aware of only a small handful of high profile lawsuits and I personally know no one who has been sued as a dog professional. And the fact that insurance policy rates for dog professionals are surprisingly low suggests that insurance companies do not experience a high rate of liability protection claims. But there certainly is more risk in working with dogs than making and selling pottery, and it makes sense to protect yourself and your business.

For one thing, if you do happen to find yourself on the unpleasant end of a lawsuit, the financial, professional, and emotional results could be very damaging. Lawsuits are stressful and can be costly. For another, we live in a litigious society. As our profession grows and the media continues to highlight and sensationalize dog bites, public awareness increases as well, and some people will always be influenced by sensationalism. In fact, more worrisome to me than the actual statistics of lawsuits are the anecdotal signs that lawyers are seeing dog bites as potentially lucrative. I remember seeing the front cover of a large California Bay Area phone book proclaiming the services of a father-and-daughter law team specializing in dog bite cases. Clearly they smell an income growth area and their enthusiasm may prove contagious.

Still, there's no need to worry. A few simple steps now and you'll have the peace of mind to fully enjoy your work with dogs. And yes, if you've been in business for a while—even years—you can simply make the changes now and be more secure. Protecting yourself is easy and there is simply no good reason not to.

Think of the three steps you can take to protect your liability as three layers of safety nets you rig between yourself and any legal trouble. You'll want your nets arranged in descending order of strength: contracts, insurance, and limited liability company status.

Contracts

A good contract with every client is your first safety net. A strong contract includes two things: (1) a section specifying any key information about the dog and the care you are to provide; and (2) effective waiver language that clearly spells out what you are and are not responsible for.

The key information might include things like medical issues, behavioral issues, the specific services you will perform, and your policies—payment, cancellation, scheduling, etc. (More on policies in Chapter 7.) Have yourself and your client sign off on anything that could be a potential issue in the future. For example, food allergies, behavioral problems, or service details. It would be a shame to find out too late that a dog in your care was allergic to chicken or was fearful of and likely to snap at children, or that a client was expecting you to take their dog for two walks a day when you thought you were to provide one. Worse yet would be a client who claimed he told you about the allergy or behavior problem or their two-walk expectation when you know different. A good contract, then, is a legal record of what you did and did not know, as well as what you and the client agreed to.

The waiver language portion of the contract is language spelling out the areas of responsibility held by you and by your client. Typically this section has specific legal language that protects you in the event of accidental damage to the dog or any persons.

To obtain a good contract with legal waiver language, you can contact friendly colleagues to see if they might be willing to share theirs, have a lawyer draft one for you, or purchase a contract from a professional organization that supports dog pros (see Resources).

However you obtain one, it is always a good idea to have your attorney go through the contract to make sure it is as tight and effective as possible for your specific use and in your state. This approach is far less expensive than having a lawyer draft the paperwork from scratch.

A few tips:

- Use a contract with every client.
- Use a fresh contract when old clients come back for additional services.
- Make sure both you and the client sign and date the contract.
- Keep your contracts filed in a safe place.

Although contracts are important, they are only your first line of defense. For better or worse, our country affords all citizens the right to sue and no matter how strong a contract is, understand a person cannot sign away this right. Nonetheless contracts act as an excellent deterrent. Many people don't realize having signed a contract does not limit their legal recourse and those who do also typically understand that having signed the contract renders their arguments much weaker. It's hard for a client to claim she told a trainer her dog was reactive to children when the "Behavior Issues" section of the contract she signed is blank! Should a problem arise, the presence of a signed contract lowers the chances of actually going to court or having to pay for any real or perceived damages.

Insurance

Sometimes we make mistakes despite our best intentions. So in addition to contracts, all dog pros should have a strong insurance policy. Insurance is your second safety net should the first one fail. Luckily, and perhaps surprisingly, dog pro insurance is easy to obtain and remarkably low-cost.

A million dollars in liability coverage costs roughly $500 per year for dog walkers, pet sitters, and trainers operating without a training facility. Daycares, boarding facilities, and training schools should expect to pay roughly $1,000 per year. This cost is stunningly low considering the perception of our industry as high risk, and especially given the protection and peace of mind insurance affords.

To clarify, liability insurance covers risks for your work as a dog pro. It is separate from any personal medical insurance you carry and from any homeowner's or renter's policies. I am often asked if liability insurance can be obtained through a homeowner's or renter's policy. Unfortunately the answer is no.

A final, important word on liability insurance—not all policies are created equal. Check any policy you're considering for two issues—breed restrictions and coverage "after contract." Some insurance companies have tried to exempt breeds considered higher risk from their policies. So you're covered so long as an incident doesn't involve, say, a Pit Bull or Rottweiler or Doberman or whatever other breeds the company deems dangerous. Fortunately, most insurance companies backed off this stance a few years ago when they found dog pros cancelling their policies in favor of companies covering all breeds. Still, it doesn't hurt to double check.

The most crucial difference among policies is that many do not cover "after contract." Imagine a couple hires you to help with their dog, Benji. Benji is lovely but is dog reactive when walked on leash. You spend a number of sessions working with Benji and her people. Two months after your last session Benji has a dog-dog incident while out on a walk and the result is a redirected bite to the other dog's owner, who got his hand too close to the fray. The other dog's owner sues Benji's parents, who in turn sue you, claiming they were following your instructions when the bite happened. Perhaps your lawyer advises you to settle and you turn to your insurance company for support, only to find that the fine print clearly (or not so clearly, as the case may be!) states that your policy covers only while you are under active contract with a client. The lesson is to be careful when choosing your insurance carrier—ask whether a policy covers after contract. And don't assume that because a prominent professional organization promotes a particular company that their policy covers after contract—they may not. Additional insurance information can be found in the Resources.

Limited liability companies

Becoming a limited liability company (LLC) is your third available safety net. The most common way to be in business is as a sole proprietor or partnership. A sole proprietorship is a business owned by one person and it is the default mode of doing business. If you don't actively decide to be something else, you're automatically a sole proprietor. A partnership is the same thing, but with more than one person.

The chief advantage of being a sole proprietor or partnership is simplicity. As with any business you'll need a license and a fictitious business name, and should carry insurance. You'll have to keep track of your financial records and pay taxes. But that's it—there's no other paperwork and it is the simplest form of business for taxes, too—what the business makes, you make. What the business loses, you report as a loss. Pretty simple.

But the simplicity of doing business as a sole proprietor or partnership has its downside, too. The law and the IRS see a sole proprietor and her business as the same legal entity. That's why taxes and paperwork are so minimal. But being a single legal entity also means that when the business is in trouble, you are, too. If there's a lawsuit it's not just your business assets at risk—it's anything you own personally, putting your property, trust fund, savings, investments, etc., at risk. When selling widgets this risk is minimal. Working with animals with teeth is a little dicier.

To avoid this risk many businesses organize themselves as corporations. Unlike sole proprietorships or partnerships, corporations are considered separate legal entities from their owners. If the business encounters trouble it stays with the business. A protective brick wall, if you will, is raised between business people and their corporations, affording liability protection and potential tax breaks. Unfortunately corporations come with a major disadvantage for most dog businesses: they are complicated to run, as they are required in most states to have a board of directors that meets and files minutes at least once per year, and to issue stock to stock holders. This is a lot more work and hassle than most dog trainers are interested in. And if you don't follow through on these matters properly your protective brick wall crumbles. You can't just file a corporation application—you have to act like a corporation to be treated like one.

Fortunately, since the late 1980s the LLC has been sanctioned in all 50 states as a way to help small and medium-sized businesses enjoy the advantages of sole proprietorships and corporations without the disadvantages of either. An LLC delivers the simplicity and the liability protection in one package.

LLCs are simple to form and can consist of just one person or many. Each state has its own application form and fees. The application form is rarely longer than two pages. Fees vary widely from state to state—from $40-$500. Some states have yearly renewal fees, some do not. Most yearly renewal fees are low. (California residents have the added burden of an $800/year state tax.) By default, LLCs are taxed the same way as a sole proprietorship, but you can opt to be taxed as a corporation. Consult a tax accountant familiar with small businesses, LLCs, and corporations to find the right taxation scheme for you. This is best done before becoming an LLC, as part of determining whether it's the best option for you, and to make sure you have the information you need to act properly as an LLC. LLCs have far fewer requirements than a corporation, but they must be followed for the safety net to work.

Given the fees involved in your state (or the tax in CA), should you become an LLC? Only you can answer that, but here are some things to consider:

- What is your risk level? Are you pet sitting cats in their homes or teaching puppy classes? Or are you walking dogs off leash or working aggression cases?

- What do you stand to lose? Are you just out of college with little to your name, ready to launch your first career? Or are you married with a home and retirement investments, pursuing your dream job?

- What is your risk comfort level? Are you the trainer who believes the lawsuit will never find you, of all people? Or are you the dog walker who worries each night before falling into a fretful sleep that tomorrow will be the day?

Put your answers to each of these questions in one hand, and the fees involved in your state in the other, and judge which feels heaviest. If you decide to pursue LLC status, search for your state's secretary of state website—you'll almost certainly find a downloadable application there. You will also find additional resources in the back of this book.

CASE STUDY

Sharon and Rebecca traded notes after the LLC workshop. Sharon leaned toward transitioning her business to an LLC. "With the kids getting ready for college and the house almost paid off— it just seems like a good idea. I think I would feel safer with my aggression cases, for sure." Rebecca, just out of college, had a different perspective. "I don't know," she told Sharon. "I think I'll just be a sole proprietor, especially while I'm only doing puppy classes. I'm not making enough to worry about yet, and I can't imagine anyone would want my lame old car! I don't think my pockets are deep enough to worry about!"

What to do if you've been operating without all this stuff

What if you've been in business for a while without all this in place? No reason to fret—you can remedy the situation now. But don't delay. Setting aside the time is a bother, the fees are irksome, and facing the paperwork can be stressful. But the greater professionalism and peace of mind are well worth it.

Here are some tips for catching up on the issues covered in this chapter:

Business license

This is probably the trickiest item to get after the fact. I'd advise you to call the city (anonymously) and find out what their policy is for retroactive business licenses. If it looks like you'll have a large fee to pay you can decide whether to apply with your original start date or from this date forward.

FBN/ABN/DBA

Find out first whether your county has fees for filing late. Most likely they do not, but knowing this ahead of time can inform what date you use on your paperwork.

Service marks

There is no issue with filing now, as this process is optional. The only consequence in delaying is that someone else might file for the same name before you do.

FEIN

The only potential problem here is if you have hired employees without properly reporting them, but that would fall outside the scope of this book. See the Resources for additional information on this issue.

Contracts

Just start using them as soon as possible. The only consequence of not having used them up until now is that you aren't as well covered should something come up with a past client.

Insurance

You can apply for insurance at any time. There will be no retroactive fees unless, that is, you can convince your agent to insure you retroactively.

LLC

There is no consequence to filing now other than not being as well protected in the past as you will be in the future. You can convert an existing sole proprietorship or partnership into an LLC any time you wish.

CASE STUDY
Tai spent the morning screwing up her courage for the phone call. "Well, I've been walking dogs for about four years. My business is doing well and I really enjoy it, but, well..." Here she took a deep breath. "Okay, I've never had a business license or insurance or anything like that. I don't even know for sure what I'm supposed to have. I didn't mean to go so long without doing all this stuff. I just didn't get to it and then time passed and then I was afraid to find out what I should have done and how much trouble I'd be in that I hadn't. But I worry all the time while I'm out there with the dogs and I just can't take it anymore!" I was happy to tell Tai that it was not too late to put legal requirements and liability protections in place. With some support she got everything in order in no time. Now Tai enjoys her daily hikes with the dogs without her daily worries.

Order of operations: When to do what
In the Resources there are annotated To-Do Lists, with all the steps from this and others chapters laid out in order.

The order of operations is important because some paperwork requires that other paperwork has been filed first. For example, your city business license form may ask for your FBN certification—or it may be the other way around in your county. So download all paperwork and instructions and read through for cross-references. The To-Do List at the back will give you the most standard and conservative order to follow.

4

Build It and They Will Come?
You Need a Marketing Plan!

Common wisdom holds that only 10 to 20% of businesses in the United States survive their first two years. But data from the Bureau of Labor Statistics tell a better story—that 44% of businesses are still in operation after four years. That's good news, but you still have to make sure you're on the right side of that statistic. One crucial element that sets those 44% apart from the rest is good marketing, a concept that involves a lot more than printing up a stack of business cards to leave around town. You need to develop an effective marketing message, including a visual look for your business, and a plan for getting that message out there. But marketing doesn't have to be intimidating, complicated, or costly—it just needs to be creative and thoughtful. And most importantly, it needs to be done.

Find your message
To build a marketing plan, you need to know what you have to offer. How will you convince dog owners that you are the dog pro they need? Existing isn't good enough—you have to give them a reason to call you.

Marketing maxim #1: Find your niche
What makes you special? One of the most common marketing mistakes dog pros make is to generalize. If you're the only game in town, it makes sense to tell potential clients that you do it all. But if there are multiple dog pros in your area, what will make a client call you instead of someone else? Don't leave it to chance. Give them a reason to call you by marketing a specialization. Find a niche and fill it well.

First, take a look at what the competition in your area is doing. Think about what you might have to offer that is different. For example, do you have any skills from a former career or hobby that might serve as a nice complement to your services? If you are an avid runner you might offer dog runs for young, rowdy, athletic dogs instead of walks. Or a previous career working with children might be applied to a dog training business focused on working with families. Consider your preferences, too. Do you enjoy working with puppies or small dogs? Is there a training issue you are particularly good at handling? Who are your ideal clients? You might also consider any services not currently being offered that could be of use to dog owners in your area, such as pick up and drop off services, group dog walks, or small dog playgroups.

Having a niche gives a subsection of potential clients a reason to call you over other service providers in your area. These clients then tell their friends and families and co-workers about you, and you begin to build your business. Of course you can absolutely be a generalist, too. Say you're a trainer specializing in treating separation anxiety, and your marketing efforts predictably bring you clients with separation anxiety problems. If you help solve those problems, it is likely the client will refer friends and family to you for any training needs they have. Even with a particularly narrow niche focus you can expect a good portion of your clients to fall outside your specialty.

CASE STUDIES

Cindy had burned out working as a vet tech in a high-pressure vet hospital, and decided to start her own pet sitting business. The number of people already pet sitting in her area intimidated her, but her vet tech expertise made her worries unnecessary. She directed her business at owners with older and ill pets, explaining that she would be able to care both for their emotional and physical well being, including administering medicines, IVs, and any other home medical care required. She networked with veterinary offices and other pet sitters and was soon overwhelmed with referrals for clients needing special care for their elderly, infirm, or injured animals while away.

Ruth Anne found her skills as a dog trainer very useful while preparing her young dog for the arrival of her first baby and after she brought the baby home. She noticed several of the women in her new moms' group were struggling with their dogs and babies, and a niche was born. Ruth Anne changed the name of her business to Beagles and Babies and began marketing to expecting and new moms through groups, pediatricians, and the Infant and Parent Group program at her two local hospitals. She also developed curricula for two public dog training classes, one for expecting parents and one for new parents. Her business is thriving.

Before moving to the city, Margot owned a successful home-based dog training and boarding business. After getting married and moving to a small place in a big city, Margot wondered how she would make board and train work. Then she noticed all the small dogs coming and going from the high-end apartment and condominium complexes around the city. Margot built a business around training and boarding services for small dogs only. Her marketing plan included networking with local small dog rescue groups, groomers, and high-end doggie boutique stores. Her message of special care for the smalls, which included a home-like environment and healthy training treats, hit home with small dog owners and she now maintains a wait list for her services.

A word on business names

It's hard to find a name that says it all, especially if you offer multiple services. It's worth spending some time searching for the perfect fit, but don't obsess, and don't allow it to distract or delay you. The marketing you do and the quality of your service will far outweigh the importance of your name. Far more important than an ingenious name is to find a niche and market to it.

Some dog pros opt to use their own names rather than a business name. That's fine, too. Both approaches have advantages. A personal name suggests direct service. A business name carries the connotation of an established, professional company.

Marketing maxim #2: Market to your clients, not yourself

Remember that your marketing message is for your potential clients—be sure to please them, rather than yourself. Because we dog pros are so passionate about what we do, it's a universal mistake to forget clients when building a marketing message. For example, you might feel strongly about teaching people to train their own dogs. But before using the slogan "We Train You to Train Fido," stop to think whether that is what your potential clientele is looking for. Similarly, I often see dog training websites built around the notion of helping people to improve their relationships with their dogs. But again, is that what the average dog owner is thinking about when they decide to look for a trainer? Most people hire a trainer because they have a problem they want solved—a behavior they want stopped or one they wish they had more of. If you find a way to let potential clients know you can help to solve their problem, they're more likely to hire you. And once they hire you, you'll have your chance to teach them how to train their own dog, and to positively impact their relationship with him. The point is: don't confuse your goals with your marketing message.

CASE STUDY

Maria's website announced that she helped dog owners "build a terrific relationship" with their dogs. It was a beautiful website and her proclaimed goal was no doubt a worthy one. Still, though she watched the visit count to her site rise, she found that few of her visitors called or emailed. Given Maria's specialization in aggression cases, she had a strong niche to put to work. So she re-focused her website and other materials around the message of efficient and effective problem solving to meet client goals. Now both Maria and her phone find themselves quite a bit busier, and Maria is achieving her goal of helping people with their aggressive dogs—and their relationships with them.

You might make an exception to this rule if you have a strong desire to pre-screen clients for certain messages or services. For example, if you only want to work with people looking for a trainer to help them train their own dogs, rather than clients looking to have their dogs trained for them, then "We Train You to Train Fido" is a great marketing message.

CASE STUDY

During the first couple years of owning her training business, Denise was surprised to find the work so emotionally taxing. She was uncomfortable discussing training methodologies with potential clients, and got upset with clients who were not sold on positive reinforcement (R+) approaches. By the end of her second year she considered leaving the profession, even though she loved training. Instead she changed all her marketing materials to very clearly state her R+ approach. Now, most dog owners who call her are searching specifically for a positive trainer, and Denise is able to enjoy her work again.

Marketing maxim #3: Emphasize benefits

Don't just tell people what you do. Tell them why they should work with you. A list of services isn't nearly as compelling as a list of benefits. Instead of telling potential clients in a bullet point that you treat separation anxiety, ask them to imagine being able to safely leave their dog at home while they enjoy an evening out. Instead of telling them you walk dogs, point out that using a dog walker means having a calm dog to come home to after work. It's easy to forget to do this. When I first started dog*tec our tagline was "Continuing Education. Professional Support." Contrast that with "Our business is to help yours succeed." Our first try listed what we do in the vaguest of terms, whereas the revision communicates the benefit—a successful business.

Marketing maxim #4: Know your audience

Knowing your market is an important part of choosing an effective marketing message and visual identity. Who are the clients you're hoping will call you? Are they men, women, families, seniors, young professionals, college educated, middle class? What do they need—

problem behaviors fixed or a polite social dog, a quick potty break or a well exercised dog, someone to check in on their pup, or someone to stay overnight? Where do you find them? Where do they get their dog information? Where do they hang out? What do they read? Finding out as much of this information as possible will help you to make informed marketing decisions. You may enjoy designs that are on the pink girly side, but if your potential clients are primarily middle-aged professionals you might want to go for something more upscale and gender neutral. And if you know that the majority of your potential clients will be families with children you might consider incorporating that information into your marketing plan by focusing on helping families discover the Lassie in their Lab, Lhasa, or mutt.

CASE STUDY

David did his homework. Upon learning that his neighborhood church was 2,500 families strong with a high median income and lots of dog ownership, David contacted the minister about a humane education program for children and families. Teaching his program on Sunday afternoons created terrific exposure and helped to establish David as the local dog expert, eventually leading to a steady stream of clients.

For most dog pro businesses, a formal market study isn't necessary. Just take a look around and do some thinking. For example, it's easy to find out the median income in your area with a quick Internet search or call to the local chamber of commerce. But you can also look at the houses people live in and the cars they drive to draw conclusions about socio-economic status. If you require accurate statistics for a formal business plan for funding, there are website services that can help. See the Resources at the back of the book.

Another approach is to decide who you want your clients to be, and then gear your materials toward that profile. You may, for example, decide you want to concentrate on the most affluent members of your community. Or if you prefer to work with families, let that guide you.

Having said all this, make certain you please yourself, too. Don't opt for a message or look that doesn't appeal to you—it's hard to sell something you don't buy!

CASE STUDY

Wendy found her dog walking niche not in a particular type of service or dog, but in her potential client base. Looking around her community she found that among all the various groups, those identifying themselves gay had the highest income, highest dog ownership, and the highest spending per dog. "They seemed like the perfect clients to me—dedicated to their dogs and able to afford services for them." So she targeted her marketing through the local gay newspaper and dog-oriented businesses in targeted neighborhoods, to good effect. She has a terrific referral rate and is enjoying her work. "I love my clients," Wendy says. "They are enthusiastic, educated, and devoted to their dogs!"

Get the word out

Marketing maxim #5: Market!

You now have a message. But what do you do with it? How do you get the word out there? Although you can grow a business by unprompted word of mouth alone, it takes a long time. Somebody has to do the talking, after all, and how will you get that first wave of clients?

This is where most businesses fly or fail. The fifth maxim of marketing, the most important one, is simple enough: You have to market yourself. Too many dog pros make up a few business cards, leave them around town, and then wait for the phone to ring. But there is an ocean of business cards strewn around coffee shops and pet supply stores—how many of them do you pay attention to?

What to do, then? Begin by considering your strengths—what do you do well and enjoy? Are you a good public speaker? Are you better working with small groups or as a one-on-one teacher? How's your writing? What about your planning skills?

Now consider your environment. What other dog-related businesses are around? Vets, groomers, supply stores and boutiques, shelters and rescue groups? Oh—and don't forget other trainers, walkers, daycare, and sitters, too! They can be a terrific networking resource. What about local activities? Are there dog parks or local festivals, adult education or community classes? And what are local folks reading—any local dailies or weeklies or monthlies? In short, what's going on in your target neighborhood?

CASE STUDY

Robert had just graduated from dog training school and was contemplating the intimidating task of starting a new training business in a market saturated with dog trainers and walkers. On top of that, he wasn't yet feeling confident enough in his training skills to just jump in. But a good niche coupled with professional networking solved both problems. Robert set up a business walking difficult dogs, dogs not behaviorally suitable for other walkers and daycares. And, rather than marketing directly to the public, he marketed to the other trainers, walkers, and daycare businesses in the area. Soon he had a full schedule of dogs referred by daycares and fellow walkers and trainers.

Marketing maxim #6: Use creativity, not cash

You've got your niche, a list of your strengths, and a list of local places and activities. Now it's time to get creative.

This brings us to our sixth marketing maxim: Creativity over cash. It's not that money can't be a great help to a marketing plan—of course it can—but most dog pros don't possess large amounts of start-up capital. And the reality is that a little cash doesn't go a long way in marketing. So if you don't have the big bucks, your creativity can stand in nicely.

As you scan your two lists, you're looking for good potential match ups between your skill sets on the one side and the resources or potential opportunities on the other. If you enjoy writing, perhaps the local neighborhood weekly would like to run a regular "Ask the

Trainer" column. A dog walker with good writing skills might offer an article about the benefits of dog walking, a pet sitter on how to pick a sitter. What terrific exposure, at no cost! And so much more effective than running an ad, especially when you're attempting to sell yourself. A column establishes your expertise and credibility. You become the sought-after local expert. Or, if you're a trainer specializing in helping people with puppies and new dogs, wouldn't it be great if the local shelter recommended you to all of their adopters?

CASE STUDIES

Tasha couldn't help notice as she walked her pack of client dogs every day how messy the dog park had gotten—trash, untended piles of feces—it was unsightly and, she felt, gave dogs, dog owners, and dog professionals a bad name. Seeing an opportunity to do something for her community and her dog walking business, she worked with the parks department to co-sponsor, organize, and promote a Dog Park Clean Up Day. The park got cleaned up, her business got lots of free press, including an article in the local paper and a short spot on the local evening news, and Tasha got several new clients.

Hilary had been trying for some time to network with her local shelter. The shelter had good standing in the community and was viewed as a source of training and veterinary knowledge, but they did not provide private training services. She knew they were short staffed and thought both she and they could benefit from a referral service. She decided to leave her cards on the front desk counter, but it seemed they were rarely given out, and she hardly ever received referrals. Then she offered to help answer the shelter behavior hotline. Together with the behavior manager, she set up a triage system for incoming calls to take pressure off the shelter staff. They determined which calls the staff could easily handle and forwarded the more difficult ones to Hilary. Hilary was careful to limit the time of each

call, providing some immediately applicable management advice, and then scheduling a consult
with anyone interested. The hotline is now Hilary's
number one source of clients.

Marketing maxim #7: Create relationships

Writing a local column and getting shelter referrals are great marketing goals—but how do you make these things happen?

This brings us to another oft-made mistake in marketing dog pro
businesses: Asking instead of giving. As I said before, the typical marketing plan includes drawing up business cards or brochures to post
around other dog-oriented businesses. Often dog pros ask the business owners for permission to place cards on their bulletin boards or
brochures in a holder on their counters. If brave enough, a dog pro
might even introduce herself, talk a little about what she does, and
ask for their referrals.

But ask yourself: from the business's perspective, why should they
give referrals? They don't know you and aren't familiar with your
abilities, they're busy, and asking for a favor gives them no motivation to help. The trick is to stop asking for help and consider instead
what you might have to offer.

If you'd like to write a regular column in the neighborhood paper,
first try offering one article, already written, on a dog topic of broad
interest. If you would like the shelter to refer their new adopters to
you, put together a free adopter's package of articles or tip handouts
that the shelter can give to its adopters. Make sure your name and
business information is on all the handouts, and include any of your
other marketing material as well. And maybe they would appreciate
some training for their staff or volunteers—a small series of talks or
hands-on seminars. These offerings allow the shelter to get to know
you, to come to see you as an expert, and to build loyalty to you.
Sure, you can leave your cards on the front counter and hope people
pick them up and call, but you'll no doubt receive many more phone
calls if the shelter staff is actively and enthusiastically sending adopters your way. And if you offer a free monthly or quarterly talk for
new doggie parents, so much the better—this is a direct opportunity
for face time with potential clients!

CASE STUDY

Suzanne believed that an ounce of prevention was worth a pound of cure, especially when it comes to puppies and newly adopted dogs. She wanted to focus her business on getting people and dogs off on the right paw, but how to get the word out? The local shelter did a brisk adoption business, and Suzanne decided to start there. She offered to teach a free adopter's class at the shelter, at no cost to them. She gave the two-hour talk one evening each month, and the shelter scheduled that month's adopters into the lecture. Suzanne's talk covered the basics of setting up a home for a new dog, house training, and prevention of common behavior problems, and she always made sure to talk about her private training services as well. Her business grew steadily as she signed up occasional clients at the talks, and found that over time people who had attended her class called as they developed training problems, and often referred friends and family to her as well.

Marketing maxim #8: Be active, not passive

One reason giving a community talk or answering a shelter hotline are much more powerful marketing tools than simply placing brochures around town or an ad in the paper are that they are examples of active marketing—opportunities for clients to interact with your business rather than just seeing it advertised. Instead of picking up a business card, a shelter staffer hands your materials to potential clients while telling them, "You have to call this trainer. She is amazing and can help you fix this problem." Posting a flier on a bulletin board provides no potential for active interaction between your business and your hoped-for clients. If instead you disseminate a quarterly newsletter to the same businesses, the people who pick it up get an interactive experience with your business. The flier might have listed "problem behavior solving" as one of your services, but an article in each newsletter can highlight an issue and tell the story of one or more dogs and clients whose lives were changed by your training. Through that narrative they get to "see" an example of the benefits of your training and imagine themselves getting similar help, rather than just reading a bullet point. Think "show, don't tell."

A word about print advertising

Not only is print advertising passive marketing, it is also expensive and generally provides a low return on investment—meaning that it doesn't work that well. Although there are some exceptions, I generally advise you try other avenues first. Why not do something that is free, active, and more likely to work— and work continuously over time? You might be an exception if you have a small local neighborhood paper, as there is less chance for your ad to get lost in all the information, and because people sometimes feel more loyalty toward small local businesses. Even so, an article would give you much more mileage—and it's free. Another exception would be if other dog pros in your area all advertise in one paper—in that case you might want a presence there, too. But an article would still trump all those ads.

If you do decide to try print advertising, follow these three guidelines for success: Make sure your ad emphasizes benefits over product (remember Maxim #3!). Run your ad at least three times—repeat contact is key in print advertising. And be sure to keep track of any hits you get from the ad so you can gauge its success and decide whether to continue running it.

The success of phone book ads seems to vary, largely depending on whether you work in a competitive area. Traditional yellow page ads generally work best for dog pros in smaller communities with less competition and an older clientele. In a more saturated market a phone book ad can lead to plenty of phone ringing, but most of these inquiries are fishing expeditions—people comparing prices—that don't turn into business. If you live in an urban spot full of dog professionals it's more likely that serious potential clients will find you through active referrals from friends, family, and other dog businesses such as vets, retail stores, other dog pros, or shelters, or by coming across your active marketing projects like articles, newsletters, or community lectures, or via an Internet search.

Marketing maxim #9: Tell them again and again

A brochure is always the same. If I've picked it up once, I'm unlikely to pick it up again. Even if I do, there is no new input. A newsletter, on the other hand, encourages me to pick it up multiple times a year. Each time I read an article about a featured client and her dog I get another picture of what training, daycare, walking, or sitting could do for me, and a deepening sense of the writer as an expert. And a regular "Tips" article that I find interesting or helpful gives me a reason to hang onto my copies, maybe even tack one to the fridge. Six months from now, when I find myself struggling with a new dog problem, I know who to call, and I'm more likely to find a copy of the newsletter around my house for the phone number than a business card (if I even remember that I had the card). Or when my neighbor or friend or colleague mentions how much trouble their new puppy is, or how their dog is so bored during the day, I might tell them about the great dog pro who writes the newsletter I always pick up at my favorite coffee shop or at my vet's office.

Implement your marketing plan

Once you have your marketing plan, it's time to put it to work!

Marketing maxim #10: Develop materials for your plan, not the other way around

One of the first things many dog pros do upon deciding to start a business is to launch a website and have business cards and brochures made, before doing any real thinking about the marketing plan itself. A common result? A website in need of updating almost before it's finished, and boxes of brochures stored under the bed. And it doesn't make sense to order brochures unless your marketing plan includes a clear role for them to play.

Once you've developed a message and designed some strategies to get that message out, you're ready to decide what materials you need and what they should look like and say.

CASE STUDY

Barbara was excited about starting her business. She wanted to get things going right away. The first thing she did was hire a designer to help her with a logo, business cards, and a beautiful brochure, and a website developer to create her site. Two years later she's saving money for an expensive site over-haul, and most of her brochures are gathering dust in her office closet. They look great, but she just hasn't had many opportunities to use them. As it turns out, most of her clients come from the training classes she set up through the local Parks and Recreation Department and the local community college, and then eventually from the referrals from those clients. Parks and Rec and the college do most of the pro-motion for her classes and they're nearly always full, so she hasn't had much need for the brochures.

Let your marketing strategies determine what materials you will need. If you've decided to write a newsletter, you need a newsletter template. If you've decided to provide adopter's packets to the local shelter, you might have stickers made to go on the front of the folders that hold your articles and tip sheets, and a tip sheet template. Only get what you really need. Don't waste your resources purchasing materials that don't play a clear role in your marketing plan. Don't assume you need brochures just because everyone else has them.

Marketing maxim #11: Launch a website

Regardless of what other materials you have, it always makes sense to have a web presence. For most dog pros, a small, simple website will do. Around 5 pages (home, about, a page for each service, and a contact page) is plenty. As long as it looks polished and professional and you've presented your marketing message clearly, a simple site will get the job done for you. Don't feel the need to have a large site unless it makes sense for your business and marketing plan. If you are opening a facility that offers multiple services, a more extensive site, perhaps featuring a class and events calendar and registration capability, will save you time.

Marketing maxim #12: Don't do it yourself

Once you're clear about what you need, it's time to put together your design team. You'll need a good graphic designer to create your logo and overall brand feel, and to create any physical marketing materials your plan requires. You'll need a professional website writer to craft your marketing message into an effectively written site. And you'll need a website designer and developer (sometimes the same person, often two people who work as a team) to create the look of your pages and then turn them into an actual live website. Depending on the services your website design team offers and your level of competition, you may also benefit from hiring a search engine optimization (SEO) specialist to help your website come up higher in local searches. Each of these people plays a critical role in the success of your business. You may be tempted to cut corners and save a little money here, but it would be a false savings. We live in an Internet savvy world and people can easily tell the difference between professional and homemade. First impressions matter, and whether fair or rational or not, potential clients are less likely to choose a dog pro whose materials appear the latter.

Ask to see sample work from anyone you consider adding to your team. Do an Internet search or take a look at the Resources in the back of this book for free referrals to companies and designers who work specifically with dog businesses. You may be lucky enough to have a friend or family member who does graphic design work. But that luck comes with a downside, too, and be forewarned: I've worked with many clients suffering the frustration of waiting (and waiting and waiting) for that friend or brother or husband to finish their design work. Very often, no matter how sincere the friend or relative is, other more pressing matters will end up on top of their to-do list and the waiting ends in hiring a professional after all.

Once you find a designer, share your marketing message and strategies with her, and explain the materials you need. Typically a designer will show you a few ideas or paths to choose from and from there you select one to fine-tune.

Marketing maxim #13: Giving instead of asking—make your offers

Once you have your materials it's time to start making the connections that will turn into your referral relationships. Remember when you contact people and businesses that you are a colleague with something of benefit to offer them. You're working toward a mutually beneficial goal. You are not a start-up asking plaintively for help. You have something valuable to offer.

How do you make the first contact? It all depends on the situation, but these days the answer is often email. Email has several advantages. It allows you time to deliberate on your language and get things just right. It eliminates the discomfort of a cold call or drop-in visit. It reaches the intended person at a time when he or she has time to consider it—presumably if people are reading email it's because they have a few quiet moments to do so. A first contact by email might be particularly good for contacting newspapers, veterinary offices, and other dog pros. In addition to introducing what you have to offer, ask for a good time to call or possibly to set up a time to talk by phone or in person.

Whatever format it takes, be sure to follow up that first contact if you don't hear back. Don't assume people aren't interested—life is busy and sometimes things get in the way of responding quickly. So email again or call or, if appropriate, drop by to follow up.

Marketing maxim #14: Keep your message on target

As you carry out your marketing plan, stay on target with your message. Just as in working with dogs, consistency is key to success. Everything you do or say, and all of your visual and written materials, should reinforce your marketing message. A strong message will pull people in. Materials in which the message is weak or non-existent are a wasted opportunity.

CASE STUDY

A tragic childhood accident brought a therapy dog into Lora's world, strongly influencing the course of her life and future career as a dog trainer. She featured the story prominently on her website and in her marketing materials, feeling that it could help clients form a personal connection with her. She eventually realized, though, that her story overshadowed her marketing message and the services she had to offer. She moved her story off her home page, and emphasized her ability to help people solve tough behavioral problems. On the Services page she focused on her services, and on the About the Trainer page her professional qualifications got the spotlight, with a shortened version of her story afterward. Although she had a compelling story to tell, Lora came to understand that potential clients seek a trainer to help them solve their own problems and that the best way to get those clients was to show them she was available to listen to their stories.

One tip for keeping your message strong is to be as succinct and to-the-point as possible. There are probably many things you could say about your business, but too many competing concepts drown out the central message.

Your marketing is only as strong as your weakest message point. Consider all the opportunities potential clients have to come into contact with your business—physical materials such as cards, newsletters, fliers, and the like, word-of-mouth referrals, seeing your car go by with advertising panels, your outgoing phone message, your website, hearing you lecture, reading something you've written, and so on—these are message points. You want all of these to be polished, professional, and on target—even one off-message point can discourage a potential client.

CASE STUDY

Debbie had all her marketing message ducks in a row—almost. Her website was beautifully designed. Her truck was always clean, allowing the signs on the side to announce her business. Her business cards were professionally done, her newsletter well written. And all were on target, broadcasting professionalism. Why, then, were there so few messages in her voice mail box? Finally, Debbie understood.

She tossed out her old outgoing greeting: "Hi, this is Debbie, Stan, Maggie the Dog and Bill the Cat! We're sorry we can't come to the phone right now. For Debbie or Stan, press 1. For Maggie or Bill, press 2. If you need pet sitting, press 3. Have a super day!" She opted instead for a more professional tone: "You've reached Good Dog Pet Sitting. We're out caring for animals now, but look forward to returning your call today. Please leave your name and number, and let us know how we can help care for your good dog." Debbie finds there are far fewer clicks on her answering machine these days.

Marketing maxim #15: Reinforce referrals

A little positive reinforcement goes a long way. Don't forget to reinforce referrals, whether from clients, other businesses you've networked with, family, or friends. As trainers know, timing matters, so develop a plan right now and gather whatever materials you will need. Thank-you cards in your stationery drawer are much easier to send than ones that are still at the store. You might also offer occasional small thank-you gifts—a small gift certificate or token. Be creative here, too—for example, perhaps a local pet supply store or boutique would like the opportunity to supply you with some gift certificates or coupons specifically for your clients, at no cost to you. It could be a nice marketing opportunity for them to bring people into their store—offering a $5 gift certificate could turn into a much larger sale for them, and maybe even a regular customer. And in return you are developing another marketing relationship that will likely become a source of referrals.

Marketing maxim #16: Engage support

Though it is probably the most important thing you can do for your business, marketing is often the last task on a dog pro's list, one that is rarely checked off. Working with dog pros across the country, I've noted several reasons that keep people from marketing their businesses:

- A lack of ideas. Hopefully this chapter has helped you to develop some effective and creative ideas to market your business.

- A lack of time. There's no getting around this one. You have to make the time. The good news is that time well spent now while building or growing your business means strong word-of-mouth later. Take a look at the section on scheduling in Chapter 10 for ideas about how to create marketing time for yourself.

- Marketing is scary and intimidating. Dog pros by and large are terrifically competent and intelligent people, so why should marketing be so hard? Because, like all humans, we fear rejection. It's uncomfortable to walk into a vet's office and ask for their referrals because they might say no. That is one of the benefits of active marketing: You don't have to walk in and risk rejection because you aren't asking for anything—you're approaching as a colleague to offer a valuable service.

- Fear of failure. Most of us carry this with us to some degree. You have to be a risk-taker to start a business. I've seen clients find all sorts of ways to drag their heels—revisiting already made decisions, deciding they want a different color scheme than the one already on their cards, "taking a break" until after the holidays or to get ready for the holidays or because they need to find a new accountant or "just have too much going on." For many, the mind creates roadblocks to protect itself from the risk of failure. But no risk, no gain. At some point, you have to take the plunge.

But you don't have to plunge alone. Look for ways you might provide yourself some support as you take on your marketing tasks. Perhaps you can assemble a Think Tank group of colleagues or friends who would be good sounding boards for your ideas. Set deadlines for yourself. If you've scheduled a date to present a body language talk to a veterinarian's staff, you'll have to have your PowerPoint done by that date. Look around for classes or seminars geared towards marketing a training business, and consider engaging professional support as well. Working with a business coach can make a huge difference in creating and fleshing out ideas, helping with strategies for making initial contacts with other businesses (including developing language that feels comfortable to you), and carrying out implementation of your marketing plan.

Is it working? Track your marketing success
Marketing maxim #17: Track your ROI

You'll be putting a lot of work and time into your marketing, and probably a bit of money, too. Don't waste either on efforts that don't bring you results. A simple plan for tracking ROI—return on investment—saves time and frustration, so make sure to ask everyone who calls you where they heard about your business and keep track of their answers. Note which callers turned into actual clients—there is no point continuing a marketing strategy that brings in the wrong people. ROI tracking can be a simple matter of keeping a tracking sheet by the phone—you can find a sample in the Resources.

CASE STUDY

At first Kate was delighted by the response to her phone book ad. Yes, it had cost a lot, but the phone sure was ringing! She kept track of the number of calls that came from people seeing the ad—the number was more than she'd dared hoped for. But a few months later Kate wasn't feeling nearly as enthusiastic. Her record keeping revealed that very few of the phone book ad calls were turning into clients! Because she was paying attention, she was able to reassess her ad and decided to put her money and time into a more effective marketing strategy.

Another reason to track ROI is to fend off doubts and discouragement. I often see clients decide that something isn't working when they've simply had a bad week. After examining the data they realize things are coming along well—and the sense of being in control, having one's finger on the pulse of the business, makes them feel better, too.

Lastly, don't forget to give each of your marketing efforts enough time to work—few show an impact right away. People take time to think and make a decision. That's why repeated contacts are a marketing rule. Six months is a minimum before you can reasonably expect to judge the effect of any given strategy or project, and giving each effort a full year is best.

5

Online Marketing Basics

In the last chapter we focused on marketing basics and applying a set of maxims for general marketing success. Now we turn specifically to your online marketing presence. Many of your potential clients will search for dog services online, and you want them to find you when they do. And nearly all of them—whether they initially find you online, or via a professional referral or one from a friend, or by reading your article about life as a dog walker or your print newsletter or hearing you speak about aggression—will explore your company online before they decide to hire you. Be sure what they find there convinces them they've found the right dog pro.

Website basics

Let's face it: some websites are better than others. Just like in the real world, the details make a difference. Strobe lights and high-decibel Lady Gaga set the right tone for a teen girl's clothing store, but would be less successful at the maternity shop down the street. When it comes to your own site, you'll need to hit the right people with the right message. Here are some tips for making the most of your virtual presence.

Website maxim #1: Don't do it yourself

I said it in the last chapter, but this bears repeating. You wouldn't build a brick-and-mortar store with your own two hands. And yet the Internet is littered with homemade sites poorly designed, written, and coded. For a dog owner wondering which local pro to trust with their beloved companion, a site designed and written by professionals implies a level of across-the-board competence, making the choice clear.

Graphic designers give your site the right look, pleasing to the eye and aligned with your brand. Writers craft messages with a big marketing punch, choosing words that all at once convey information, engage the viewer's emotions, and push your site closer to the top of search engine results. And web designers bring it all together in one quick-loading, well-coded whole.

Hiring the pros does cost money. But in an increasingly web-savvy world, your site should be the last place you cut corners. Keep the rest of these maxims in mind as you work with your website team.

Website maxim #2: Retire the dancing Chihuahua

Blinking smiley faces, background music, videos that launch themselves, and where's-the-pause-button slide shows frustrate viewers, and detract from the capable, professional image you want to project. Good photos work better than animated gifs while still offering visual variety. If you insist on adding moving parts to your site, let your visitor control them with a click.

Website maxim #3: Less really is more

People don't read websites like they read books. Your potential client will scan your page, then zero in on the relevant info. Nothing provokes the urge to click away and check one's email like a long page of unbroken text. Hold your potential client's attention with short paragraphs, bullet points, and lists.

Website maxim #4: Give them what they want

Potential clients will move on to the next site if you make it hard to find what they're looking for. Make critical information easy to access.

In addition to carrying your marketing message, your homepage should provide:

- Business name
- Location/areas served
- Summary of services you offer
- Phone/email

Create a separate "About" page for staff bios; a page for each of your services, describing them in greater (though not long-winded) detail and providing your rates; and a final "Contact" page. Use clear and consistent navigation links throughout.

Include contact information—a phone number and active email link—on every page in an easy-to-find location. The top right-hand corner is best, and it doesn't hurt to place them at the bottom of each page, too.

Website maxim #5: Let others sing your praises

With Internet shoppers giving greater weight to customer reviews, grit your teeth and call in a few favors. A "Testimonials" page, with detailed before-and-after success stories ("I can finally walk Bowser by the neighbor's dog!") is worth its virtual weight in gold. Sprinkle short testimonial excerpts throughout your site, too, set apart visually to draw the eye. (And this is something you can do right from the start, while you're saving up enough endorsements for a full page.) Consumers know that some businesses fake their own praise, and reviews signed with full names and locations sound more authentic than those signed "Tricia K."

Website maxim #6: Write in lay-speak

You pursue continuing education in canine behavior. You network with other dog pros and subscribe to industry email groups. You know the lingo. Your clients don't. Few will have more than a vague understanding of the term "positive reinforcement," let alone "R+." Whether it's "recall," "sep anx," or "resource guarding," be sure your writer chooses words with the dog owner in mind. Choosing words your potential clients are likely to use will also help Google match your site to their searches.

Website maxim #7: Show them who you are

Your professionally written and designed site will show off your professionalism and give potential clients the basic information they need about you and your services. But if you can, take one step further to show off your knowledge, skills, and personality by sharing useful content and insights into what you do and how you do it. Add a blog or an area for articles if you're a strong writer. Create videos of yourself or the dogs under your care in action. Or link to your Facebook page or other social media outlets. These website additions give people a more intimate and direct way to experience you and your business. They speak to your passion for what you do, share your expertise, give people insight into what hiring you would be like for themselves and their dog. For a potential client sitting on the fence, a little extra content can be just the thing to convince them to pick up the phone or shoot you an email.

Website maxim #8: Keep on message and stay off the soapbox

We talked about marketing messages in the last chapter, and nowhere is it more important to stay on target than on your website. Your website is for your clients. Their priorities are different than yours. Most owners love their dogs, but they've chosen career paths that don't leave their hands smelling like liver treats at the end of the day. When owners steal five minutes in their cubicles to surf the Internet for local dog pros, they're not worried about the quality of their human-canine bond or out to improve their relationship with their dog. They just want to come home to an intact couch and a still-white carpet. They're short on time and need their dogs walked, groomed, or trained not to jump up on attractive neighbors. So be sure your website answers two questions:

1. Where does it hurt?

2. And how can I help?

In other words, your website should be focused on how you can help dog owners. Will you give them peace of mind by caring for their pets while they're away? Make their days easier by walking the dog for them so they can come home and relax with a tired-out companion? Solve the frustration and embarrassment of being pulled down the street when they do walk the dog themselves?

And avoid the temptation to use your site to lecture on proper training methods or the exercise needs of young Labradors or the responsibility of the dog owner to learn how to communicate better with her dog. Because an owner is like her dogs in at least one respect—neither of them like to be scolded. You can summarize the key benefits of R+ in brief and welcoming prose. You can talk about how working with you will help their dog become responsive, or how a daily walk or romp at daycare will make their dog calmer and easier to live with. Don't confuse your goals for clients with your marketing message, and don't forget your website is a marketing tool, first and foremost. You'll be better able to change a client's behavior *after* you've been hired.

With these tips and the right professional team in place, your site will make a formidable first impression, setting you apart from other local dog pros and grabbing the attention of potential clients. Good design, strong writing, and a clean layout will quickly provide the info clients need, earning their gratitude and trust.

Social media basics

It's easy to get swept up in the social media craze and buy into the notion that it's a panacea for marketing success, that if you just launch a Facebook page, business will come marching your way. Unfortunately it's not quite that simple. Social media can play an effective role in your marketing plan, but avoid the temptation to put all your marketing eggs—and hopes—into this one basket, especially in the early stages of your business. This makes sense when you understand how social media works, particularly in our industry.

How social media works

Most people aren't trawling the Internet looking for dog pros to follow or friend. If someone becomes your Facebook fan or Twitter follower, it's most likely he or she already knows you. That person is a client, or possibly a serious potential client looking to learn a bit more about you. In short, social media in our industry is largely about retention marketing. It plays to the folks already on your side by maintaining contact and reinforcing their loyalty to your daycare or pet sitters or training classes.

As such, social media can't be actively relied on to bring new business your way on its own. Like word of mouth, it takes a while to build a social media presence to the point where you begin generating new business, particularly when you consider what small-volume businesses dog grooming or training are. (You will take on a relatively small number of clients over the life of your business compared to the volume of people a retail shop or manufacturer might see, for example.)

But staying in touch with current and past clients is valuable in itself to keep clients loyal to your services, let them know about new services you may choose to offer, and keep you in their minds. They are more likely to refer others to you if their relationship with you is strong and active—and that's in part where the new business will eventually come from. And as I mentioned before, potential clients searching for the right dog pro may be persuaded to engage your services after getting a better sense of what you're about from reading your posts or tweets or blog, watching your videos, or enjoying your photos of dogs in action.

CASE STUDY

Martha had been hard at work trying to build her business for a good eight months. She had set up a Facebook page and Twitter account, and was using Instagram to send out anecdotes from the daycare floor. Problem was, she was still only averaging three dogs per day, and those numbers weren't going to cut it much longer. I explained to her that we needed to add some offline marketing to her routine, that she was doing a great job with her social media marketing, but there weren't enough people paying attention yet. We chose projects suited to her strengths and skills—a print newsletter and How to Choose Your Dog's Daycare flyer to start with—to drive more traffic to her online efforts. Sure enough, once these community marketing pieces were in play, Martha began to see her social media followers increase— and her average number of dogs not long after.

Which social media tools to use

With this in mind, let's consider a few of the best social media options. New social media tools are launched all the time, but social media is a time-consuming endeavor to do properly, so pick and choose your outlets carefully. Here are some of the best bets for dog pros.

Facebook is the current king of social media sites, a network of one billion users (at the time of writing) who create online profiles, link to friends old and new, and share news, photos, and videos. Create a fan page for your business, and use it to share updates or information that others might find helpful or entertaining. Keep in mind the "social" in social media; unlike more traditional marketing methods, the businesses most successful at social media eschew self-promotion and instead concentrate on building relationships. The focus shifts to the consumer, and solving her problems. Provide the occasional free article on building the perfect recall or getting off on the right paw with a new puppy, point out a fellow pet sitter's site when your holiday boarding schedule is full, or answer a question about your holiday policies.

A **blog** is a website featuring regular posts, or updates, and is an excellent tool for growing your brand. Many domain hosts make blogging easy, featuring easy integration with blogging platforms like Wordpress, Tumblr, or Blogger—platforms that take care of the programming for you; just write a quick post, then hit Publish. In fact, more and more businesses set up their websites on one of these content management system (CMS) platforms. Wordpress, for example, includes a sophisticated set of plug-ins, or tools, that can improve your SEO, tag your posts with relevant keywords, and keep track of your number of visitors. Frequently updated blogs attract the most visitors, and a blog that looks neglected or abandoned may leave potential clients questioning your follow through, so budget enough time to blog at least once per week. Include links to helpful articles by respected peers in your industry, photos from the daycare floor, or funny stories of dogs you've been walking. Let your writing reflect your own speaking style; a casual, personable writing voice is more likely to attract loyal readers and potential clients.

Twitter is the social network for short attention spans, a running stream of tweets (posts) of 140 characters or less. Other users can choose to follow your tweets, which will show up on their stream. Social media is better at strengthening existing relationships than attracting new ones, and Twitter makes it easy to open dialogues, both public and private, with clients and other dog pros. Again, limit self-promotion to about 15% of your overall posts, or you run the risk of getting tuned out. Answer a frequently asked question, tell a joke, post a quick free training tip, or share info about a favorite trail or walking route. Follow and comment on the tweets of peers in the dog professions, check up on current and former clients, and you'll strengthen those connections most likely to give you the best word of mouth.

LinkedIn focuses on professional networking. Users create profiles that resemble employment resumes, and link to friends, co-workers, and employers, both current and past. Link to your grooming peers, the owner of your favorite daycare or boarding facility, or fellow students from your dog walking academy or training school.

YouTube is a massive online library for videos and can be a terrific resource for introducing your business to potential clients. Videos are also a powerful search engine optimization tool to help people find you first. YouTube videos run the full spectrum of production values, and with the popularity of video editing software, you can throw together your own short video on your computer in a few hours. Share a typical day on the daycare floor or out on the trail, or a profile of one of your training dogs and her people to show the positive effect your private training service has had on both. Never underestimate the appeal of cute dogs; videos that go viral (i.e., become insanely popular, widely linked to, and distributed by fans online) often feature animals. Create a profile with a link to your business site and embed your videos on your blog or Facebook fan page.

Flickr is an online photo and video management and sharing application. You can upload photos to the site via numerous methods and share them with clients or the public. Other users can comment on your photos or subscribe to your photo stream. Tag your photos of just-groomed dogs, dogs relaxing happily while Mom and Dad are away, or videos of the perfect recall with relevant keywords and then embed them on your business site.

Pinterest is a visual content-sharing service that allows you to share your interests, inspirations, and expertise by "pinning" (i.e., posting) images, videos, and articles to so-called pinboards. Think of it as social storyboarding or a show-and-tell bonanza. Each board is a themed collection of images about anything that interests or inspires you: dog products you love (you can go to town and have a board for each product: beds, food, collars and leashes, treats, etc.), dog statistics, holiday-themed boards (Santa Paws, Easter Dogs, Howl-O-Ween Dogs), famous dogs, covers of great dog books, a meet-the-team board with photos of you and any staff members, photos from dog park cleanups or other events, or photos from your favorite rescue group or local shelter. When the subject matter (dogs!) is so utterly interesting and photogenic, the possibilities are endless. You can post your own photos and, as most people do, also find interesting images and informative content on other sites or Pinterest streams. This is a fun and wildly popular service where dog lovers number in the millions.

Instagram is another image-based social media platform on the rise. What began as a fun way to pass pictures, videos, and short messages to friends and family is fast becoming the new thing in social media marketing. Instagram is particularly suited to dog pros, allowing you to easily share the day's walking and daycare adventures, training breakthroughs, or grooming results with clients and followers as they happen on the Instagram network and other social networks including Facebook, Twitter and Flickr. Set up an Instagram profile for your business, then share pictures of dogs having a great time and videos of them frolicking, along with caption-length messages: "It's Spot's first day in daycare—here he is making friends with Fido." Or "Watch as Fido walks past another dog, fully focused on his trainer!"

Make the most of your social media efforts

Social media for your business isn't the same as engaging in it for fun or to keep in touch with what family and friends are up to. Online marketing requires the same care as the rest of your marketing plan. Here are some tips to make your social media time pay off.

Social media maxim #1: Be sure it's right for you

One of the most common questions I get about social media is "Should I?" It depends. The two most important factors are time and interest. Some choices are more intensive (Twitter and blogging, for example) than others (such as LinkedIn). But all demand regular attention if they are to have any impact.

So if you aren't interested—if you aren't likely to actively engage in the process, if you don't like to spend time on the computer, if you're not "into" it, you'd be better served spending more time on non-social media forms of marketing. But if you enjoy social media and can commit the time, there are some potential rewards to be had.

Social media maxim #2: Don't rely on social media too heavily

Even top social media marketing gurus agree, social media is no replacement for on-the-ground marketing. Social media is something you add to your marketing plan, not something you replace it with. Spend just as much time, if not more, on non-social media forms of marketing—launch a print newsletter, invite a local reporter to join you on a dog walk, give a small number of free class passes to local veterinary clinics, etc. In short, revisit the last chapter for ideas to spread awareness of your business while you wait for your online following to grow.

Social media maxim #3: Have a strategy

Like any type of marketing, social media should be tackled with a strategy. Think about your content before you begin. Have 25 to 50 blog topics brainstormed before you start a blog. Create a list of content categories for Facebook before you launch your page, and a list of places to look for that content. Set aside time in your schedule each week to hunt for and create content to ensure your social media presence will be active and consistent. Your goal is to build and maintain brand loyalty, and it's easy to undermine it instead with inconsistency. A blog or Twitter feed that hasn't been updated in weeks looks unprofessional and implies a poorly run business.

Social media maxim #4: Be useful and entertaining

Remember that social media is about engagement, entertainment, and a bit of education. Keep the content about your services to a minimum—no more than 15%—or you risk sounding like a commercial and losing fans and followers. Think about how you can show what you do while entertaining and being useful to your audience. Trainers, share quick training tips. Walkers, share pictures and anecdotes from your day and give walking-related equipment tips and information. Sitters and boarding facilities, show the dogs in your care having a good time and tell people how to help their dogs prepare for time away from home. All dog pros, tell your followers which dog-related and dog-friendly businesses and products you recommend, flag upcoming dog events and national dog-themed days, pass on information about dogs or dog issues from the local, national, or even international news, and search out the best dog jokes, cutest dog photos, and funniest dog stories on the Internet.

For the 15% of your content specific to your services, keep the direct service entreaties (asking for referrals or letting people know about your new classes, for example) rare. Find ways to show-don't-tell about your services. For example, share fun stories from life on the daycare floor or out walking dogs, or tell a training success story. Post pictures and videos and profiles of the dogs in your care that your clients might be inclined to pass on to their friends and family and co-workers for a little bragging time.

Social media maxim #5: Be social

Part of your job is to engage with your audience, to get them talking, asking questions, commenting on your posts and each other's. Check your social media tools daily to stay actively engaged in the conversation yourself. Answer questions promptly and thank people for positive comments. Go a step further with tricks like posting questions and polls for your followers: Where are their favorite weekend walking spots? Where should you take the puppies you're training for their socialization tomorrow? Guess the breed(s) of this dog?

CASE STUDIES

Pete told me he was worried about having our marketing conversation. I asked why. "Well, I know you kind of have to do Facebook these days if you're going to have a successful business, and I'm not so much a techie." I assured Pete Facebook wouldn't be necessary and that, in fact, if he didn't enjoy it, it would probably be a bad idea. What we wanted were marketing projects right for him. "Phew, that's good news," Pete said. "All my friends have been telling me I had to do it. I probably would have started sooner if I'd known that weren't true." Pete and I chose marketing projects right for him, using the marketing maxims from Chapter 4, and he's now enjoying his retirement career as a successful dog walker.

Shay put in lots of hours on her social media marketing, but they were erratic—multiple posts on some days, long dry spells in between. Making matters worse, her content was dry. A self-proclaimed behavior geek, she tended to post long articles on training techniques, behavior studies full of techie language, and excerpts from esoteric conversations with other dog trainers. Suffice it to say she had a strong online following of fellow dog trainers, but little traction among current or potential clients. Shay set up a separate Facebook page and Twitter account for marketing purposes, and we put together a new social media content strategy, one that focused on short training tips offered in easy-to-understand lay language, fun dog-oriented cartoons, quick polls about her followers' dogs, interesting factoids about dogs, and great info about local deals and activities for dog lovers. Shay now has a loyal following of clients and potential ones, and is beginning to get new business from her online efforts.

E-Newsletter basics

Email marketing gets overshadowed by social media a lot these days, which is a great shame because email is a terrific marketing workhorse—free or low-cost, targeted, and much less time-intensive than social media.

Why an e-newsletter?

Here are four reasons you should put out an email newsletter:

1. **Sell your services.** Being front-of-mind increases the likelihood of sales. Yes, existing clients know what you offer and can use your services whenever they need to. But so many things vie for time, attention, and resources these days it's easy to be forgotten. Getting back on people's radar can mean getting back on their priority list.

2. **Get repeat business.** Clients are a built-in audience for new services. Already loyal to you, they're the most likely to try the latest thing you've added. Assuming they'll find out through other channels is risky, and people are more likely to respond to a direct message from someone they know.

3. **Build customer loyalty.** People like to feel special. Checking in creates a sense of community and increases brand loyalty, which means you're the one they come to when they need dog-related services.

4. **Get referrals.** The combination of brand loyalty and a gentle nudge that you are there makes it more likely clients will think to refer a fellow dog lover to you. If their experience with your company is buried in the past, referral opportunities are easily missed. Staying in your clients' consciousness keeps you on the tip of their tongues.

E-newsletter maxim #1: Be useful and entertaining

We talked about this regarding social media content, and it applies to email (and print) newsletters, too. If you don't offer education, information, and entertainment, people won't keep reading. If you talk too much about your business and services you're writing a glorified brochure, not a newsletter. Yes, these topics belong in your newsletter. Of course. But unless you also include articles of general interest people will soon treat your newsletter as they would any other advertising material: Maybe a glance, then the trash button. Your end of the deal is to entertain and inform, not just sell your services.

E-newsletter maxim #2: Sell your services

Though you want to avoid too much focus on your business, the purpose of the newsletter is to promote your business. Don't make the mistake of not including information about your services—particularly their benefits. Make contact information—website, email, and phone—clearly visible. Don't hesitate to include a call to action. For example, "Fall classes are filling quickly—sign up now!" Or "The holidays are just around the corner—make your boarding reservations early to ensure your dog's spot with us."

E-newsletter maxim #3: Keep it short

E-newsletters are as important to online marketing as the print version is to on-the-ground marketing, but the format is a bit different. Rather than the two- or four-page quarterly print version, your email newsletter should be monthly and short. Share a quick tip, or an excerpt from an interesting article about dogs, or a humorous or thoughtful anecdote from one of your walks. Put together a fun profile of one of your daycare dogs, complete with a picture. Include a short call for referrals to friends and family or a schedule of upcoming classes. That's it. Keeping each e-newsletter short and entertaining means clients are more likely to read the next one—and hopefully to pass it along, too.

E-newsletter maxim #4: Actively build your list

You're going to put some work into getting your newsletter out each month, so the more people reading it the better. First of all, have a prominently displayed sign-up field on your website. Also include a "Forward to a Friend" button in the newsletter itself. Most email marketing services (and you should always use a service, such as Constant Contact or Mail Chimp, for example) offer this option as standard.

Also include a benefits-oriented call to sign up for your newsletter on all your materials, however mundane. Class sign-up sheets, handouts, brochures, postcards, rack cards, even business cards and invoices. Include it in your email signature and on your stationery. If you write an article for a local paper, mention it in your bio blurb. If you are on Twitter, tweet about an interesting newsletter item and link to the sign-up box on your site. On Facebook, post the entire newsletter and include a sign-up box beside it (a free, downloadable application lets you do this). Ask your brick-and-mortar referral sources (vets, shelters, pet supply stores, for example) to have a sign-up sheet on their counter or in their lobby. And don't forget to include it in your printed newsletters, too. In other words, never miss an opportunity.

One more online project: Add yourself to referral sites

These national (and sometimes local) websites with built-in referral databases position themselves as the go-to place for people trying to find the best this, that, or the other. Some are large, general, and exclusive directory sites you have to apply to, that cover all manner of services. Others are referral sites focused on a particular kind of service, such as dog walking or pet sitting or training. Not everyone looking for something on the Internet will do a specific, logical search that includes their geographic location. When potential clients simply tell Google to look for "dog training" there's a good chance they'll end up on one of these referral sites, where they can then search for a trainer in their local area. If they do, they'll find you—if you're listed. It's sort of like 1-800-DENTIST for the 21st century.

Getting listed on most of these sites is free; a few come with low annual fees that are generally worthwhile. What's a $50 annual marketing expense if it gains you even one client? And having large sites with lots of traffic linked to yours can also boost your website's search rankings, helping you to appear higher on the page when people do remember to search by location. See the Resources section at the back of the book for a list of referral sites to check out.

6

Keep Them Coming Back

Though it's often a profound love of dogs that brings people to the dog services profession, most dog pros soon catch on that the human client is at the center of the business. The client lives with the dog day and night while we see them in short bursts. And then there's this reality: Dogs don't carry checkbooks and day planners. If we're going to work with dogs, and be paid for our efforts, we have to take good care of their people.

Follow up and keep in touch

Few dreams are more alluring to the small business owner than the one in which a business builds itself by word of mouth. We've all heard some version of the story: Without a marketing budget or any tedious footwork, Let Sleeping Dogs Lie Inc. grew from a garage outfit to a three-star, nationwide boarding and kenneling enterprise. Who wouldn't want that? And yet most business owners sorely neglect even the most basic cultivation of referrals, without a doubt the cheapest and easiest form of marketing available.

Your clients lead busy lives, and people are only capable of focusing on a finite number of things at once. An obvious statement, yes, but if you keep this truth in mind you can make your business and training practices more effective.

Once a client stops actively working with a trainer, his or her commitment to daily training begins to slip—especially when the training has improved a dog's behavior. As trainers we know that old, unwanted behaviors, practiced many more times than the new, will begin to resurface.

When that happens, some owners return to what you taught them and regain lost ground. But many don't have sufficient skill or understanding to do so. Hopefully they'll call you. But some won't. Perhaps they're too busy or believe the training didn't work because the same old problem is back again. Maybe they're embarrassed. Don't count on referrals from these clients. Instead, they're more likely to tell friends, "Well, we hired a trainer and it sort of seemed to work, but then Milo just started up the barking again. I'm not sure what to try next." Clearly not the type of endorsement that will bring you word-of-mouth business.

Dog walkers and daycare operators have a different challenge—your clients get so used to you being in their lives they almost forget you're there, especially if you pick up and drop off their dogs while they're working. These owners may not think to offer referrals because you do your job so well you've dropped below their daily radar.

For sitters and boarding facilities, a job well done usually means a return client. But checking in with clients from time to time keeps you in their minds, which means they're more likely to think to tell others about you. And timing your check-ins well will help clients remember to schedule early for their trips, vacations, and holidays, which is a great help to your scheduling.

Follow-up benefits
Following up with clients regularly is important. If it sounds like extra time, then yes it is, but time spent marketing your business is time spent generating business. And that's how you should think of follow-ups: it should be a standard marketing practice for you. Trainers, some of your clients will be in situations in which they need you to come back for a touch-up. Had you not checked in they might not have gotten around to calling. Because you called they got the help they needed, are happy with the ongoing results, and are more likely to tell friends and family about you.

For all dog pros, checking in briefly and respectfully with clients will keep you in their line of sight. In Chapter 4, I mentioned the importance of repeat contacts. Regular follow-ups constitute repeat contact with your clients—keeping yourself in their consciousness. Regardless of whether they need help, owners are more likely to refer someone your way if they've had recent contact with you. In other words, if you are part of the finite number of things on their minds. And your consistent concern for them helps build their loyalty.

Use a follow-up system

Decide in advance how often you want to follow up with each client. Trainers might choose to check in after two weeks, one month, three months, six months, one year, and then twice a year thereafter. Have a schedule or a spot on your weekly calendar where you note the dates for each client. Many email and online calendar programs have functions that will automatically alert you of pre-set dates and tasks. Set aside a few hours once a week at a regular time to take care of all your follow-up calls and emails for the week.

Dog walkers might choose to leave a quick hand written note or send an email or text daily to let dog parents know how much fun their dog had that day. Daycares can send home a weekly "report card" detailing each dog's most notable moments and any new accomplishments. Sitters and boarding facilities can also employ daily texts or emails and a post-stay report card as well as checking in with clients a few times a year via email or a card (or another marketing idea such as a newsletter) to remind owners to sign up early for summer vacations and holiday trips.

Practice your follow-up routine efficiently. Have rules about what you will help with over the phone and when you will suggest a follow-up appointment. Unless you want to spend hours on each phone call or engage in a long email dialogue, avoid general, open questions like "How are things going?" or "How is Toto?" Instead, help clients stay on task by asking specific questions such as, "I wanted to check in on how Toto is doing when he sees other dogs—is he looking at you instead of barking?" And once you've hit the one year mark you can choose to send cards as follow-ups instead of calling or emailing—especially if the previous check-ins have been positive. A quick handwritten card is a nice touch and takes less time than a phone call or email conversation.

Using prompts and positive reinforcement to build referrals

Another obvious but often overlooked practice is to ask for referrals. It is funny how many people don't think to offer them—even when they're happy with a service. Most likely this is another function of how many things vie for our attention in a hectic culture. By simply asking for referrals—and rewarding them—you can make a huge difference for your business.

Prompt them

You don't have to be bold or pushy to ask for a referral. Instead, watch for comfortable opportunities. When a client offers praise such as "Thank you so much—you are great! I can't believe the difference training has made!" grab the opportunity to say "Thank you—I'm so glad I could be of help to you and Clifford, and it's been such a pleasure working with you. I hope you'll let any friends, family, or co-workers with dogs know about your training experience. If you know anyone you think might benefit from training I'd be delighted to work with them." They've just told you how wonderful you are, and you're able to slip the request naturally into conversation without any worry of being rejected. And they're more likely to send referrals your way because you've introduced the notion.

Reinforce them

Reinforce every referral, and practice good timing—just like when you train. Use a system to help with efficiency and promptness. Keep a database of client contact information in one place (such as an Excel spreadsheet or professional dog business software—see Resources), stock up on thank-you cards or postcards (all the better with your business name and logo), and have a variety of thank-you tokens on hand. For example, ask a local pet supply store to provide you with coupons (a marketing opportunity for them, too). And make up coupons for your own services—a small discount off the next training class or next pet sitting, or a free day for dog walking or daycare clients. You can also send small items with your logo on them—small bags of dog treats, for example. Having many ways to say thank you is great for clients who send multiple referrals, as you don't want your gesture of appreciation to look routine.

For clients who consistently send others your way, you can streamline your reinforcement process by occasionally (two or three times per year) sending a general thank-you card and gift, not directly related to any particular referral, in which you express your gratitude for their ongoing support and share how much you enjoy working with the people in their lives. Go a little bigger for these clients—a gift basket of doggie and/or human goodies, for example.

Prompts versus lures

These suggestions are similar to using prompts and rewards in dog training—analogous, say, to a hand signal followed by a treat. In my experience, it's best to avoid outright lures with clients—offering something up front for a recommendation: "I'll give you such-and-such a discount if you send your friends to me." You may see some success from this approach, but not necessarily any more than from a prompt. Prompts lead to the first referral and your reinforcements keep them coming. This way you build loyalty—your clients suggest you because they believe in you—and that makes for stronger referrals.

It works with your marketing network, too

Finally, why not also use the ideas in this chapter to cultivate referrals from other marketing connections? Other dog professionals and services, and anyone else you are networked with, can be excellent sources of referrals. Just don't forget to return the favor whenever you can.

7

The Nuts and Bolts: Services, Rates, and Policies

Many an overworked dog pro leaves the task of defining her services, rates, and policies until the last minute, generally when some unanticipated question or problem arises. Perhaps it occurs when you are faced with a marketing decision such as choosing text for a website or flyer. Or worse, you have to scramble to come up with an off-the-cuff answer when your first client calls asking a question about how you handle cancellations. It can be embarrassing, because what, after all, should be more self-explanatory than the services of a dog trainer or walker, right? It seems simple, but if there is a lack of clarity about the services you provide and, even more importantly, the ones you don't, you leave yourself open to misunderstandings and confusions, perhaps outright conflict. You also run the risk of your business running you, instead of the other way around, as clients end up dictating your services and policies simply by default. The time spent now defining your services, their costs, and the resultant policies is guaranteed to spare you many future headaches. See the Service Comparison chart in the Resources for more details as well.

Training services
If you are starting a training business, there are a number of service-related issues you need to clearly define.

1. What training issues do you cover? Do you work on basic obedience, puppy issues, basic behavior problems like impulse control issues, serious issues such as shy or fearful dogs and aggression, or competition training including obedience or sports? Is there a behavior issue or type of training

you will not work on? For example, are you comfortable working with aggression? If so, in what forms and at what severity? For example, will you work cases with a bite history or with children in the house?

2. What kind of dogs will you work with? Do you have limitations on size or breed or age of the dogs you're willing to take on?

3. What kind of support services will you offer? Will you be available by phone or email to answer follow-up questions? And if so, will you charge for this or build it into your rates? How will you place boundaries around such a support service? Will you offer written homework notes? If so, will you write them on the spot, or type them up and email them?

4. Will you work directly with your human clients or train their dogs for them? Will you train privately or in groups?

Let's look at this last issue in more detail. Your basic options are coaching, day training, board and train, and public classes.

Coaching

In the last couple of decades this has become the standard format for positive-based trainers. Because positive-based trainers place so much emphasis on changing the way people understand and interact with their dogs, training the people rather than the dogs has become a mantra. Focusing on training the owner has a lot of advantages, chiefly because the training is done in the context of the home and by the client—meaning the dog responds to the owner instead of the trainer. Many clients like this method since it usually costs less than board and train situations, and the owner gets to keep his dog with him during the process.

But one drawback is that coaching can be a slow process. The reason for this is not, as is sometimes assumed, that positive methods are inherently slow, but rather that it takes a lot of time to train humans. As trainers we are faced with the challenge of trying, typically in one-hour segments once a week, to train people to do the highly skilled work that we ourselves learned over a much longer time period and in much more concentrated doses.

Where basic obedience and puppy raising are concerned, there is much to be gained in return for the time invested. And in-home training is a must for issues that require a behavior modification plan with a large management component, such as digging, chewing, counter surfing, jumping on guests, watch dog barking, housetraining, and separation anxiety. For these problems, teaching the owner to do the training is optimal because the work needs to happen in the context of the dog's everyday life. Coaching clients in their own homes also allows trainers to design plans that take into account the client's routines and environment, thus increasing the likelihood of compliance and success.

But the issue becomes muddled when we consider complicated behavior modification techniques for serious issues. Should we be teaching such techniques to guardians for self-implementation? Lack of essential training skills, consistency, and perseverance on the part of the guardian often lead him or her to give up before any discernable progress has been made. And while a flimsy recall or intermittent sit hurts only the guardian's pride, dog-dog aggression left untreated could have serious consequences. Some behavioral issues are generally best left to the professionals when possible. After all, does a lawyer teach a client how to argue a case himself? Does a doctor teach a patient how to do his or her own operation?

Coaching is best suited for trainers with highly developed teaching/coaching and interpersonal skills, and for clients who enjoy working with their dogs (versus those who "just want the problem solved") and who exhibit strong mechanical skills. Many will also prefer it for the lower cost, though that lower cost in most cases also comes with weaker outcomes. After all, the less training done—and the less of it done by a dog trainer focused on proofing—the weaker the results are likely to be.

Day training
Day training as a category falls somewhere between coaching and board and train. The trainer trains the dog in the dog's home (or wherever the problem is occurring or the client wishes to see reliability—at her workplace, the park, out and about town, etc.), and then teaches the human client the required skills and concepts to maintain the training.

One advantage of day training is schedule flexibility, as training the dog can be done during the day and doesn't require the owner to be present. Another, that you often see faster progress than with coaching because a professional trainer can get more done in the same number of hours, and is more likely to effectively proof behavior.

Such speedy and lasting improvement is in itself thrilling to a guardian and rarely fails to spark a high level of engagement, but compliance often increases too, because the effort required to maintain the training is less than what would be needed for the client to train to that level herself. Another advantage to day training is that trainers make more money from fewer clients. The fast-spinning revolving door is a central challenge for dog training businesses. There is very little recurring income in training. You get a client, you address their training goals, and then you must find someone to replace them. Day training slows the revolving door down. Rather than seeing each client once a week and leaving them to do the training in between, day trainers typically schedule four sessions per week for each client—three training sessions with the dog and a transfer session with the owner. Thus day trainers need far fewer clients to maintain their schedule and income. Finally, your client may appreciate the convenience of having her doggie goals addressed while she's at work or running errands.

The central disadvantage of day training from a client's perspective is that it typically comes with a larger price tag than coaching. On the other hand, the training is done much faster (day training cases typically resolve in three to four weeks), the results are much stronger, and someone else—you—does all the heavy lifting for them.

All obedience (and especially issues that demand more practice time such as leash manners) and long-winded, highly technical problems like fear and aggression lend themselves particularly well to this format. And even training issues like jumping on guests and separation anxiety, which require a strong coaching component, can benefit from a hybrid approach that includes day training to lay foundation behaviors more quickly.

Day training works best for trainers who enjoy flexible scheduling and lots of hands-on time with dogs. You will still need excellent coaching skills to teach the concepts and mechanics necessary to keep new behaviors strong and/or old behaviors at bay, though many trainers find teaching maintenance easier than coaching behavior modification from the beginning. Partly this is because the level of skill the clients need to attain is less. Much is also likely due to the owner's reduced anxiety levels and the strong buy-in that come with seeing the trainer's results. Clients who have less time than money or who require more immediate results may prefer day training.

Day training can also be done in a facility setting. Trainers who run a facility can opt to have clients drop their dogs off on the way to work, and trainers without the overhead of a facility may wish to partner with a local daycare or two, offering the daycare clients the option of paying extra for daytime training sessions. Make sure that this option comes with mandatory transfer sessions, just as in the home environment, so the dog and client learn to work together to maintain the progress you make.

Board and train

If you are able to house dogs in your home or at your facility, board and train can be a very lucrative option. There is a sizeable market segment of people willing and able to pay a premium for the convenience and expediency of having a dog taken away and returned without the behavior problem or with new behaviors ready to go. Of course, one or two appointments at a minimum are required in which you teach the guardian how to maintain the new results in her home. Other benefits of board and train are that you can work with the dog at your own convenience, and that it can be a quicker approach than coaching and day training, given that you have many more trial opportunities daily than you would if you worked with the dog in his own home.

Board and train works well for obedience, basic manners, and aggression. Like day training, however, it is not as effective for behaviors such as destruction, counter surfing etc., for which management in the dog's home environment is a key component of the training plan.

Trainers who enjoy working directly with dogs and who prefer fewer coaching hours may find board and train particularly satisfying. Still, as with day training, teaching skills are crucial for transferring the results from your house or facility to that of your clients. Owners with the available capital who need faster results (or who travel frequently and want to get more from their boarding buck) may appreciate being able to send Fido on over to your place.

Group classes

Classes are great for basic obedience and fun activities such as sports and tricks, and puppy classes are an essential modern component of proper socialization (so long as they are run properly to avoid negative play experiences and opportunities to practice inappropriate social behaviors). On average, however, a class is not necessarily the easiest or most beneficial environment for behavior issues—an exception would be dog-dog reactivity; many trainers are generating impressive results with Growly Dog (dog-dog reactivity) classes.

The time-honored setting of a class appeals to many people, combining, as it does, a relatively inexpensive way to train a dog with a pleasant social activity. Classes also present an opportunity to spread the word about your private services.

Dog walking services

The major questions for dog walkers concern whether to walk dogs on or off leash, individually or in groups. On-leash walking of one dog at a time is the simplest, safest way to go but is also the slowest to generate revenue. Walking a group of dogs off leash together is a better revenue generator, but requires considerable skill and knowledge if it is to be done safely and well, and off-leash legal places to play—not easy to come by in many locations.

Another central matter is who you will walk. Will you take a dog with a poor recall? What about those with indecorous car manners? Do you feel safe walking a resource guarder or a dog with human aggression or dog reactivity?

From a marketing standpoint it pays to be absolutely clear about the extras you are planning to offer, if any. For example, what kind of clean up will you provide the dogs—none at all, a rub-down with a towel after a muddy walk, a hosing off in the yard, a bath once a week? Will you carry out any additional tasks, such as feeding or checking water bowl levels, maybe leaving the dogs with a Kong or other stimulation toy?

Dog sitting services

The number one question for sitters is whether to sit in the client's home or in your own. The advantage of your own home is, well, that you get to be home and can maintain much, if not all, of your normal routine, which is particularly important if you have a significant other or a family. The advantage of sitting in the pet's home is that the pet is often more comfortable and relaxed there, and many clients prefer this service—particularly if they have other animals such as fish, rabbits, birds, or reptiles that cannot easily be moved.

Another important service area to define is the precise type and extent of your sitting. Will you be staying overnight in the pet's home or dropping in—and if the latter—for how long exactly? Often a client will pay a premium to know that his or her animal is being kept company overnight but, in addition to being a time-consuming commitment, it also means that you cannot personally take on more than one client at a time.

Are you a pet sitter, a dog and cat sitter, or just a dog sitter—which animals are you comfortable caring for? Do you have the necessary knowledge and skills to, say, feed a reptile or provide mental stimulation for rats or rabbits?

Finally, will you attend to additional tasks such as watering plants (indoors and/or outdoors) and bringing in mail? The advantage is that there are clients who would gladly pay for such comprehensive services while they are away. The downside is that you may feel that such tasks undermine your professional image.

Daycare and boarding services

Will you offer just daycare, or will you also board dogs? Boarding can be very lucrative, and you have a well-primed target market at hand in your daycare patrons. On the other hand, it involves camping out overnight at your facility, which you would either have to do yourself or pay a staff member to do. Either way, the costs need to be factored into your overhead.

What will your daycare or boarding services look like? Are all the dogs in the same daycare room together all day, or will you create an itinerary to break up the day into various activities to make it more stimulating and safe for both dogs and staff? Will boarding dogs be given dog-dog playtime if temperamentally suited? What will you do for mental stimulation for those dogs who are not able to participate?

A word on a la carte services

I strongly advise against charging extra for additional services. Charging for things like providing dogs with a stuffed Kong or a chewy, outdoor playtime, a walk, a bedtime snack, or even staff cuddles (yes, I've seen this!) essentially implies to potential clients that you will only take care of their dog if paid extra to do so—that without their willingness to tack on additional charges, their dog will simply sit in her kennel all day or be ignored by daycare staff. This is a terrible marketing message, intended or not. And who wants to run or work at a dog facility where some dogs receive mental stimulation and exercise while others do not? Instead, include such things for all dogs and charge accordingly. Raising your rates to cover your overhead for physical and mental stimulation will attract higher paying clients who value the care you give their dogs.

What other services might you offer to open up new revenue streams for your business? Could you, and do you want to, offer individual training or public classes? Grooming? Retail? Dog massage? Yes, these types of services complicate your business but the more you provide the greater your potential income, and you can more readily compete with other facilities if clients see your business as a one-stop shop for their dog's needs.

Packaging your services

How you sell your service matters—a lot. Packaging services carefully encourages clients to use them more consistently, decreases sales pressure, and increases your revenue.

For dog trainers, selling up front the number of sessions or weeks of training you feel are needed to provide the best chance of reaching a client's goals is a three-way win—for you, for the client, and for the dog. To start with, you get to spend less time marketing and selling. So if you don't enjoy the role of salesperson and dislike having to sell the next session each time you meet with a client, packaging is a terrific way to lump all the selling into a one-time event. You only have to present the material and convince the potential client once, and then you can get to work. Packaging also means a better chance of receiving longer-term income from each client, as you get a full commitment up front. And you are much more likely to enjoy the satisfaction of a resolved case, because you have the time needed to get the job done.

Because she committed to enough time to complete a full training plan, the client will get the help she needs. It sounds basic but is no small boon. So many of life's interventions can get in the way of dog training—money concerns, suddenly getting too busy at work, or getting just enough relief from a problem to decide not to continue (which any trainer will tell you is a situation likely to unravel in the long term). Your client is much more likely to meet her goals if she has committed herself to the number of training sessions you recommended and has paid for them in advance. Note that I'm recommending that you, the trainer, decide the size package that is required. Offering clients a menu of packages (a three pack and a six pack, for example) often sets you, the client, and the dog up for failure. Don't give a client the option of choosing three sessions for a ten session-sized problem.

Asking clients to commit to the amount of training actually needed to reach their goals also provides you a better chance of helping the dog. If you see the client (or the dog) enough times to "fix" the problem, the dog's quality of life will likely improve significantly. We know that a well-behaved dog is more popular at home and generally safer in his dealings with the world and from threats of re-homing and euthanasia. Few things are harder for a trainer than knowing you could have helped a client meet her goals but, for whatever reason, you didn't get the chance to do so, and that falling short of those goals could mean the dog will suffer.

For walkers and daycare operators, packages guarantee regular income and are really a must. A drop-in approach to walking and daycare is a messy and inefficient business model. You never have an accurate grasp of your monthly income or staffing needs, if pick-up routes are involved they vary daily and require constant planning, and your pack composition changes every day. This adds unnecessary work for you and your staff. It's also stressful for the dogs, who must negotiate new social dynamics daily. You'll experience fewer dog-dog incidents if your packs are consistent. And packages allow you to streamline your operation for the optimum number of lucrative clients, meaning you avoid the risk of having to turn someone away because you're too full. Best to spare yourself the aggravation of having to say no to someone who wants regular care five days a week because you have too many drop-ins on Thursdays.

Some dog pros eschew packages, sometimes because the prospect of making a large sale at the outset of a client relationship is downright torturous to them, sometimes out of a fear of laying down strong policies, especially when other local businesses let clients use their services however and whenever they choose. Ultimately it is up to you. Can you overcome any squeamishness about salesmanship and policies for the higher good of your business?

Selling a training package
With obedience packages, program length is less of a concern and a client can happily choose whatever option she can afford, so long as you set the expectations for how many cues will be covered under the amount of time she chooses. But where addressing a serious

behavior issue such as resource guarding or stranger fear or dog-dog reactivity is concerned, it rarely makes sense to allow the client to choose the number of sessions herself. You, as the expert, know what needs to be done and should determine the amount of time needed. As I said before, allowing a client to choose a three session package for something you know will take at least ten sets everyone up for failure—yourself, the client, and the dog. Needless to say this doesn't make for good business, as your chances of building a strong referral base dwindle if you are not finishing cases.

So if behavior issues form part of your service menu, it is worth spending some time developing language that explains your package policy. Something along the lines of: "I would be very happy to help you with Roxie's fear of people. We should be able to make significant improvements, but stranger fear is a complex behavioral issue that takes time to address. To help you meet your goals, we will need a minimum of [insert number here] sessions. That will cost [insert cost here]. I require my clients to commit to the entire behavior modification program up front because my goal is to give you the best chance of success in meeting your goals for Roxie. It is all too tempting to give up part-way through—either because other things begin to compete for time or monetary resources, or because progress feels slow in the beginning, or because you begin to feel some relief and think, 'This is good enough.' But stopping early just about always means seeing progress unravel and old behavior surging back. I want to see you meet your goals for Roxie, and that will require time. I know this is a large commitment, and so have given you my package rate, which is a $-- discount off my regular hourly fee. If you'd like to get started I have an opening next week..."

The idea here is that you are granting a discount (it doesn't have to be large—even $5 or $10 off each hour is helpful and can make a client feel like she is saving) to offset the commitment of the package. I also recommend setting yourself up to take credit cards so that you can offer to spread the package costs out via a payment plan. But either way, the clear implication is that without a package there'll be no training. And the language centers on the client's needs and your desire and ability to help. Some clients will choose not to pay. That is okay. As you know if you're already in this business, your services won't be right for everyone. But you are more likely to make money and enjoy your business if you work with people who are truly committed. The client is more likely to reach her goals, which means you feel good and so does she, and she might even want to tell her friends about you. It is a rare client who offers a referral to a service from which she didn't see results.

As for selling a package, I recommend an initial consult with a new client first. Let them meet you and gain confidence and trust in your abilities before you suggest the financial and durative commitment of a package. With a complete interview and a chance to meet the dog and the guardian you'll also have a better idea of what size package is most appropriate.

Designing training packages

For obedience, you might offer a number of package sizes, and I recommend spending some time finding inviting or fun names, too; it helps with the marketing later on. You might also describe roughly the number of things that can be accomplished in each. For some of my clients we have created a chart inviting clients to choose a certain number of behaviors from one or another box (simple behaviors such as sit versus more long-winded ones like loose leash walking, for example), depending on the size of the package.

For behavior problems, you must obviously pinpoint the number of sessions based on what you learn in the initial client interview. What are the issues, how much time does the client have to work with the dog and how skilled does he or she seem, does the dog appear to be a fast learner or not? Choose a number you think will give you sufficient time to help the client reach his goal without jeopardizing safety and allowing for one or two training glitches along the way. You have to be honest, though; make sure you mention that there are no guarantees and that, if coaching, the guardian's success or lack thereof depends largely on his own efforts.

To keep things simple, choose a single package rate discounted from your hourly fee. For example, let's say your regular hourly fee is $100. Perhaps you charge $90 an hour whenever you require a client to commit to more than two or three sessions. So an eight session package would be 8 x $90=$720 (without a package discount, it would be $800, so the client saves $80). If you worry about doing math on the spot, carry a little chart you can refer to. I don't recommend posting these prices—simply give each client the price and discount as you explain your services. Include your initial consult price and hourly fee on your website and a statement about the availability of discounted, customized packages, but do not list package size and price details to avoid giving clients the impression that package size is up to them.

Another terrific way to sell your training services is to design specialized packages. With a puppy package, for example, you might include time for all the things you think a new puppy owner needs for success, including essential knowledge (for example, how dogs think and learn), preventative measures (bite inhibition, socialization, handling), immediate needs (such as housetraining), and obedience behaviors. Figure out the number of sessions needed and price it based on a small discount from your regular hourly fee. If you have a niche, think about how you can dress that specialization up in a package. You might wish to create two or three size options to be sure you're able, again, to provide the amount of training a client needs. For example, you might offer two day training packages for leash reactivity—say a three week option and a four, depending on the severity of the case.

CASE STUDIES

Suzanne, a dog trainer, saw many clients just once or twice, and this transient state of affairs was not only disappointing, it made running her business that much harder. Together we went through a sample of her past cases and identified a pattern—clients staying on just long enough help to smooth over whichever troubling dog behavior had caused them to contact Suzanne in the first place, and then, after experiencing some modest relief, choosing not to continue with additional sessions. All the while Suzanne knew she could offer much more, and that in all probability the target behaviors would resurface fully without additional work. To solve this problem we designed a selection of behavior packages aimed at the types of problems Suzanne saw most often. This or that package, she would explain to a potential client, was designed specifically for the type of problem he or she was faced with and, lo and behold, had an inviting discount built in as well. After several months of working with packages—getting used to selling them and so on—Suzanne saw the majority of her cases follow a healthy and predictably successful pattern, and as a result her client referrals began to climb, too.

Another dog trainer, Kip, was slowly souring on his chosen business. Every weekday evening and all through the weekend when his 9-5 friends were out and about enjoying themselves, Kip was hard at work. And that might have been all right if his clients weren't so universally resistant to completing homework assignments so that progress was slow and hard-won, particularly with behavioral issues. Rather than switching careers, he decided to switch his former one-on-one coaching practice to owner-absent day training packages. Training dogs primarily during the day left more time open to see friends, and the few hours now needed to coach clients on maintenance skills were much easier and more fulfilling for Kip than teaching clients to train from scratch. And he noticed, too, that clients responded with previously unseen enthusiasm for the work, excited by the swift changes in their dogs' behavior Kip was able to produce.

Designing walking and daycare packages

Walking and daycare packages are usually monthly affairs. Either you invoice at the end of the month based on a daily rate and the number of days each client uses (see policies, on the next page), or, ideally, you invoice for a set amount prior to the month, based on a daily rate and the number of days each client commits to. Some progressive dog walking and daycare companies are even now charging a flat rate per month for all clients—a practice beginning to gain ground and with a number of advantages, including more predictable income for you, encouragement for clients to take more advantage of your services to their own benefit and their dogs', and a nice price break for clients who use walking or daycare services full time. (This happens because pricing based on an average number of days per month comes out in the clients' favor. It's still in yours, too, because this packaging method means increased revenue from clients who otherwise would have paid for fewer days.)

The point in packaging daycare and walking services is to move away from the drop-in and pass models, which encourage clients to use services sporadically, causing staffing and cash flow issues as well as increased human and dog stress on the daycare floor or on walks, a higher degree of dog-dog incidents, and greater marketing and sales pressure. We'll continue this discussion in the Cancellation Policy section below.

What do you charge? Setting your rates

Setting rates is relatively simple and yet in my experience many dog pros find the process stressful. What it boils down to is this: in much of mainstream America, dog training, walking, sitting, daycare, and other canine services have traditionally been regarded with bemused indulgence and even low-level disdain. And to be fair, the industry has attracted and nurtured its share of eccentrics over the years, many of whom had no formal education or experience. The stubborn stereotype—of the unschooled, self-taught, largely anti-social dog trainer—and the widespread misconception that dog walking, daycare, boarding, or sitting requires no skills whatsoever may be alive and well in places, but they are wholly untrue, and every dog pro owes it to him or herself to contribute to their annihilation. In the face of this, the challenge for most business owners is believing that they can demand a good rate and that they are worth it. Well, there really is no other way for me to say this than: You are. Your services are valuable, in fact they are essential. At present, there are roughly 68 million pet dogs in America and that number is growing steadily. Without having to get into the tragic figures of dogs who are given up, re-homed, or euthanized every year due to common and highly treatable behavior issues, suffice it to say that dogs and their guardians need you. By all means charge for your professional knowledge and skill set.

To set your rates, first look at your competition. You can start with an Internet search for like businesses and then call them for additional information if needed, or ask a friend to do so if you prefer. If you are fortunate enough not to have any local competition (very rare these days!), examine the competition in an area similar to your own in terms of human, canine, and economic demographics. What are they charging? And what do they offer for those fees? How is the service similar to or different from what you plan to offer or are offering? Come up with three numbers—the lowest anyone is charging, the highest, and the most common rate.

Now look at your income needs. What is the bottom line you need to live on? How many clients would you need to have at the common local rate and at the highest local rate to make this number? Analyze this until you have a good grasp of the numbers involved.

Next, consider what your time and skills feel worth to you. Imagine yourself completing a training session or finishing a walk or a sitting appointment. Imagine the client handing you a check. Look down at the figure on the check (once you're in the car of course, not in front of the client!). It's the lowest number in your area. How does that feel? Look down again. It's the average price for your area. What does your gut say? Look one more time at the highest price paid in your area. What do you think?

Don't forget your intended audience—who are your potential clients? Are you drawing from a wealthy neighborhood, middle class suburb, or working class area?

Finally, give some thought to marketing—where on the bell curve does it make sense for your business to sit? At the bottom end, up in front, with the main pack, or somewhere in between the pack and the leader? Yes, you may get more calls if you're priced low. But do you want your clients to be bargain hunters or committed guardians? Many people find that clients who pay less have lower compliance and/or do not value the service provided them as highly. If you're priced in the middle, you'll need something that sets you apart from everyone else in the same spot (see the Niche section of Chapter 4). The psychology of charging at the top is based on the widely held American beliefs (true or not) that "you get what you pay for" and that cost equates quality. And don't forget your overall marketing message—if what makes you special in your area, for example, is being the only certified dog pro, then it wouldn't make sense to charge at the lower end.

Understand, in short, that your rates are part of your marketing message, and that you run the risk of undermining yourself by charging too little. Serious dog owners don't want the cheapest dog walker or dog trainer—they want the best. And if you undercharge, they'll likely assume that that's not you.

Consider all these factors and make a decision. Be especially careful on two counts. One, don't undersell yourself. It bears repeating that your services are valuable and worth paying for. Two, set your regular fee high enough so that when you factor in discounts you are still being paid what you want and need to make.

A word about being new

It's tempting, when first starting out as a dog pro, to aim your sights a little low. Your marketing hasn't had sufficient time to draw in business, and the phone isn't ringing. You feel maybe it wouldn't be quite right to charge as much as others with more experience. But undercharging is really never a good idea. First, you risk painting yourself into a corner. Your first training clients may refer business your way, but they're liable to share news of your low rates as well, making subsequent sales at a higher rate more difficult. And for ongoing services like daycare and walking, and repeat services like boarding and sitting, starting out low means having to raise rates for current clients sooner. You're also likely to find that your low rates attract the wrong kind of clients, bringing you bargain hunters rather than committed clients you can expect to build brand loyalty among. Which means that as soon as you do increase your rates, you'll need to look for new clientele. So rather than charging less as you start out, invest in solid education in your field up front and commit yourself to steady, ongoing continuing education. Be honest with yourself about what you do and don't know, and pass work that's beyond your experience level to more qualified colleagues. But don't apologize for being new through your rates.

Watch the discounts

Compassion for clients, copying other dog pros, and worrying about building business and making ends meet can easily lead to giving out too many discounts, which ultimately puts a business on shaky financial ground.

Remember: the central purpose of a discount should be to increase your overall revenue. Before giving a discount, ask yourself: What is the purpose of this discount? Why am I giving it? Will giving this discount drive more business my way? How? If you can't easily, soundly answer these questions, you probably shouldn't give the discount.

Avoid overly generous discounts when a much smaller one would give clients the same psychological benefit. Avoid giving discounts that are really de-facto rates. For example, if you give a class discount for rescued dogs in a community where 85% of dogs are rescued, that's not a discount—it's really just your rate.

And always avoid offering ongoing discounts that aren't actually necessary. For example, it's a common practice for daycares and walkers to offer discounted pricing based on how many days a week a client uses. A dog walker might, for example, charge $25 a day for one to two days/week, $23 for three to four days, and $20 for five days. Problem is, if you do the math I can just about guarantee such a policy is costing you a minimum of $10,000 each year—and often it is much more. What's worse, the discount serves no purpose. Clients will commit to the number of days they need, period. No one who only needs three days a week will pay for five because of such a discount—it would cost them extra per week to do so ($28 extra in the example above). If your walking rate is $25 per day, that's what you should be charging for every walk. Walking and daycare are finite volume businesses, after all. You can only walk a certain number of dogs each day, and allow a certain number of dogs onto the daycare floor. It makes no sense to offer ongoing discounts. If your competitors do so, let them make that mistake. You're better off holding out for the clients who understand the value of paying full price for your service. They'll be more loyal, and you'll make more once you're full.

Reserve the majority of your discounts for customer service uses. You might want to thank a client for their referrals of friends and families with 20% off their next class, or a free day of daycare. You can use a similar discount to show remorse over a mistake. Think of these as brand loyalty discounts. They're part of running a thoughtful, caring business. But be judicious. Handing out too many can mean significant revenue losses.

Setting effective policies (i.e., training your clients)
Having and scrupulously enforcing strong policies actively trains your clients to behave as you wish them to, and in the long run this strategy reduces the risk of conflict, saves untold amounts of exasperation, and protects your revenue. In summary, the sooner you attack this task the better.

Cancellation and vacation policies

Contrary to what we all might wish, the tricky area of cancellations can seldom be addressed with a laid-back attitude, because the consequences of last-minute or frequent cancellations deeply affects your revenue as well as your effectiveness.

Trainers, if you sell a package and the client cancels or is a no-show, he has already paid for the missed session. But if you don't reschedule, you cannot help him or his dog. There's no point selling the number of sessions you think necessary for the best chance of success if you then allow the client to miss them, regardless of whether you've been paid. One option is to charge clients for missed appointments and require that they be rescheduled. In my experience few trainers are comfortable doing this, but the process is made easier by taking credit cards. This way your policy can be to automatically charge the card for missed appointments, rather than having to ask for a check or issuing an invoice. If you've explained the policy clearly up front when the package was agreed upon, you will be able to head most cancellations off at the pass with a simple reminder when the client calls, emails, or texts to cancel: "We can cancel, yes, but before we do, a reminder that we'll need to reschedule and I'll have to charge your card for that appointment. As I explained, I only work with a small number of clients at a time, and I require all clients to commit to the full number of training sessions—it's my job to give you the best chance of success. So are you sure we can't make your original appointment time work?"

You'll find that 90% of attempted cancellations are aborted at this point, and that the client won't try to cancel again. Of course, you can always make exceptions for true emergencies—that's just good customer service. The point of a strong cancellation policy is to protect against cancellations by whim when clients are just feeling a little too busy or overscheduled.

Some trainers also implement a compliance policy. They explain to clients the importance of attending all sessions, then set a number of cancellations (should be a low number, perhaps two) that result in a forfeiture of training, with no refund for any missed or already used sessions.

It is my recommendation for walkers and daycare operators to encourage clients to use your services full time, five days per week. Short of that, use a minimum-and-set-day policy. For example, you might require all dogs to walk or attend daycare a minimum of three days per week, and on the same days each week. Invoice clients for all their days, regardless of whether they actually send their dog out. For example, if a client is on a three day per week contract, committed, say, to Mondays, Wednesdays, and Fridays, invoice based on the number of M, W, and F's in the month (or based on an average month for a flat monthly rate), even if they miss days. This has many advantages for you, your clients, and the dogs. With such a policy you can accurately predict income and any staffing needs, and keep administrative time to a minimum. You and your staff and the dogs are able to settle into a predictable routine, rather than dealing with a different mix of dogs each day. This means fewer incidents and less stress for the dogs, too. Your clients benefit from knowing that their spot is always secured—no need as you get busy to call or email or register online by Sunday night for spots next week, only to find that one or more of the days they need are full.

Understand that lost income from any cancellation—even one with reasonable notice—cannot really be replaced in these services. A cancellation policy should protect you from revenue loss. Asking for notice doesn't do that in this case. Asking for 24 or 48 or even 72 hours notice is not a cancellation policy—it's a courtesy policy. Present your minimum-and-set-days policy to your clients this way: they are paying for a spot for their dog, whether they use it or not. It's like paying for a spot for their child in daycare—you may choose to keep your child home on a given day or for a week to visit grandma, but the daycare does not give you a credit for this. You pay for the entire month whether you use it or not, because you are paying for the privilege of the spot. Gym membership is another analogy—you pay monthly for the ability to go each day. If you only go two days a week or even if you never show up, you still pay for the full month.

Some clients will balk at this idea, but most likely there is another dog walker or daycare in the area that allows drop in and will accommodate those clients. You will be better off building a business model that is sustainable and predictable, and that appeals to serious clients who understand that your services are worth what you charge and who appreciate the value and benefits of how you structure them. Consider also that this approach requires fewer clients for the same volume of business, as the drop-in model necessitates taking on many more clients to ensure a high-enough daily average, resulting also in often wild daily and seasonal fluctuations.

If this no cancellation policy makes you uncomfortable, you can soften it by giving your clients a set amount of time off, such as two weeks per year or three days per quarter or a day a month, etc. This vacation policy, which one of my clients cleverly calls "excused absence policy," acknowledges the unpredictability of life and allows clients a little breathing room. In this scenario, after a client has used up his days, he can of course still keep his dog home whenever he chooses, but he still pays for the days that are "his." Some dog pros like this approach for the flexibility it affords the client, a clear benefit to herald when marketing. Others find the adjusting of invoices a hassle and do not allow compensation for any absences.

Sitters and boarding facilities might consider using a graduated cancellation policy based on the amount of notice given. For example, if someone gives you a month's notice, is that enough time to fill the space? If so, you might offer a full refund for cancellations reported to you a month in advance. As you get closer to the sitting dates, the amount of refund diminishes. Perhaps you give a 50% refund with two weeks notice, and no refund with shorter notice. There is no correct answer here—you have to look at the likelihood of filling the space and set your policy accordingly, remembering that the point is to avoid revenue loss.

Scheduling policies

Trainers, don't allow your clients to dictate your schedule. Asking "what time is good for you?" leads to chaos for you, with small batches of time throughout the day that are difficult to put to productive use. Instead, offer pre-set appointment slots for clients to choose from. Doing so projects a successful business, and starts you out on the right foot with clients who acknowledge your status as a professional and the value of your time.

Daycare and boarding facilities, set your pick-up and drop-off times. Failing to do so means chaotic days, with restless, unsettled dogs, and more staff needed more hours of the day. Daycares, consider charging a fee for missing these times, but a fee large enough to deter, not to encourage a regular practice of arriving late. Boarders, don't allow pick-ups after a certain hour, especially if you board from home. Instead, keep the dog overnight and charge for the extra day. Your private hours are too valuable not to protect.

Dog walkers and sitters, if you ask each client for their preferred pick-up or visit time, every one will say, "noon." You can't run your business on that model. Instead, let clients know when you'll be visiting their dog, giving a time window so you can adjust your schedule and handle the unexpected as needed.

Homework and compliance policies

Trainers differ greatly in their approach to homework compliance. Flexibility on this often sensitive subject may gain you longer-term business and loyalty from busy or overwhelmed clients. The drawback, however, is your own risk of burnout, as it can be intensely frustrating to see time pass with hardly any progress made. There are trainers out there who swear by the strictest of homework policies— if you don't do it, you're fired. It comes down to personal preference, and all I generally recommend is that you think the matter over carefully, decide where you stand, and then clearly communicate your expectations to your clients at the outset of the relationship.

Aggression cases are a notable exception. Here, an ironclad homework policy can save lives and protect your business, and any trainer who takes on aggression ought to have such a policy. Say, for example, you are working with a dog who has a history of biting, and you recommend that the dog be muzzled in public. It is not safe to then leave it to the guardian to decide whether or not she feels like complying on any given day. You must insist she does, because if she is neglecting her muzzle desensitization work and/or is taking the dog outside without his muzzle on, people are at risk, the dog's life is at risk, and your own personal liability is much higher.

When clients consistently struggle to complete their homework, ask yourself first if your training plan can be adjusted to better suit their lifestyle and skills. If you've done all you can on that front, think about switching them to day training or board and train if doing so would be appropriate for their training goals and within their budget. And if you find client compliance to be a difficult or frustrating issue, all the more reason to look at day training and/or board and train as your primary mode of operation.

A note on client compliance for walkers and daycare operators: if you decide to ask a client to take care of a behavior issue say, for example, by hiring a trainer, be sure to give the client a specific timeframe in which it must be done, and be clear about any consequences of not following through.

Payment policies

I always advise my clients to ask for payment prior to the rendering of services, with the possible exception of initial training consults, which are more often paid at the time of the consult. It is just sound business. Pre-payment cuts down on repeated cancellations, secures a consistent stream of revenue, and is the only way to project income with any kind of certainty, something that is required if you ever wish to expand your business, branch into new areas, save for your retirement, or hire employees. Again, when presenting your payment policy to your clients, make it clear that their outlay reserves a space—whether in a walking group or in a daycare or in your sitting or training schedule.

Communicating and enforcing policies

Whatever policies you choose, communicate them to your clients in a frank and straightforward manner. Policies should be written into your contract and you should explain them verbally as well. It also helps to have the client initial the policy section of the contract after you've explained it verbally so there is no chance of hearing, "Well, I didn't know."

Practice your verbal delivery of all your policies. And put your marketing spin on: You have these policies in order to maintain your commitment to small walking groups, or to allow for a high daycare staff-to-dog ratio, or to allow you to take and concentrate on a small number of training cases at a time, or to keep your boarding facility small for lots of one-on-one attention. In other words, tell clients why your policies are actually good for them and their dogs.

Be clear in your mind about what action you will take if a client breaks a policy. Will you give a one-time warning, or will you enact the policy on the first infringement? If you feel that it is reasonable to give a warning, only give one and make it very clear. Say a new client cancels a dog sitting appointment. You might say, "I'm sorry to hear that Bailey won't be with us next weekend. As you know, our policy is not to give full refunds with less than a month's notice. Since you are new to us, I'm going to refund the sitting fee minus a processing charge just this time."

Changing your rates and policies

If you are reading this chapter and fretting over a lack of policies or realizing that your rates are too low, don't worry. You can make changes, even large ones. The key to smoothly changing rates or policies is to give your clients plenty of notice and clear explanation. Depending on the size of the change, you might give them several months.

Communicate the change in writing first, and yes, use old-fashioned paper and envelopes. Then follow up at least a couple of times, either by email or in person, and finally provide a reminder close to the date of the change.

In the initial letter, explain the change clearly and, if appropriate, the reasons behind it. Avoid the inclination to over-apologize or over-explain. If you worry that the change may result in some clients leaving your services, ask them early on to communicate their intentions to you. You may be surprised just how few clients choose the door. If you've done your job well a small inconvenience will not shake their loyalty. If you do lose a few clients, you will still benefit in the long run from being paid what you're worth and having clients who respect your policies.

It's a good idea in general to communicate with clients by letter periodically. Have a regular routine of communication so that bad news isn't the only time they hear from you in writing—don't accidentally create a negative CER (an unpleasant emotional response)—to hearing from you! This also allows you to have a regular routine for announcing changes or updates, which means you will more easily be able to make rate changes every couple of years to keep your rates up to date.

CASE STUDIES

Candy's dog walking rates were low for the area, but she had not raised them in years and worried about doing so now. How would she explain the change to her long-standing, loyal clients? Would they balk and go elsewhere? After doing the math, however, she knew she couldn't continue to put it off, and together we drafted a cheerful letter to her clients about how much she enjoyed their dogs. She explained the change and the reasons for it—to bring her rates in line with the current industry trend and to cover rising gas costs while allowing her to keep groups small—and said that she hoped the increase would not prove too much of a burden or inconvenience. In the end, she was overwhelmed by the response. Many of her clients emailed or called to say that they couldn't imagine their dogs' lives without her. Only one client chose to leave, and Candy realized how relieved she was—this had been her one troublesome client, always complaining about money and minute details. She soon had a new client in his place, along with a renewed sense of her work's value and a larger monthly deposit for the bank.

Judy moved across the country to take over a house and kennel she and her husband had bought to realize their dream of a quiet rural life. Her first morning in their new home, Judy watched in disbelief through the window as a truck pulled up to the kennels and a man got out and left his dog in a run, then drove off without a word. Anxious, she called the previous owner, only to find out that this casual drop-off method was par for the course—all her clients simply stopped by with a dog on a loose as-needed basis. Judy realized in that moment that taking over an existing business would not be as simple as she had hoped. After carefully drafting her policies, Judy wrote a gracious letter introducing herself to the kennel clientele. She presented the new business, including a fresh menu of services with clearly defined kennel policies, and explained the various benefits of her newfangled ways, primarily that her policies would allow her to provide the best care possible for everyone's dogs. She was happy to find that the majority of the customers were willing to comply, and that her innovative and structured way of running things began to pull people in from the nearby towns as well.

Edward specialized in separation anxiety and his training business was booming. This might have been great except that Edward rarely had a moment to stop and breathe, and strongly felt something had to change. An analysis of how he spent his time quickly revealed that far too many of his hours were eaten up by phone conversations and email replies to clients currently working on separation anxiety protocols—all without pay. The amount of money Edward was losing by not charging for this time was staggering. But what to do? His clients needed regular help and support to be successful. We retooled his separation anxiety package to include a predetermined amount of support time, based on the average client's needs, and built that time into his package price. From then on, Edward informed clients that additional time would be charged separately, and also suggested guidelines for which issues and topics were best handled with follow-up support and which were better suited to in-person work. With this change in policy, and some reworking of his schedule, Edward was soon enjoying his work again—and being paid handsomely for it.

8

Old Dogs: Growing Pains

If you have been operating a dog business successfully for a period of time, you are to be congratulated, especially if you're turning a profit. That said, while not all dog businesses develop the same way, many owners experience growing pains as the business matures. Growing pains tend to occur at several key points in the development of a dog-oriented business:

- When business is picking up, but you're still working another job as well.

- When the business has grown to such an extent that the need for better organization and efficiency becomes critical.

- When, because business is booming or because you have a need to increase revenue streams, you're faced with the decision of whether and how to expand.

- When the business is large enough that you need to bring in extra help—to take on employees, independent contractors, or partners.

I quit!—Moving from part to full time
Leaving the security of a regular paycheck to devote yourself to a full time dog business is often the first critical point as your business matures. Even if that paycheck came with mind-numbing 9 to 5 boredom, walking away from that security can be both terrifying and exhilarating.

When is it the right time to make the move? How do you know you'll be safe? There are no one-size-fits-all answers to these questions, and certainly there are no guarantees in the volatile world of self-employment, but careful planning will increase your chances of success and can help lower your anxiety levels during the transition period.

Some people are at an advantage because they have supporting income from a significant other, savings, or another source. If that is you, use it. Your business will be up and running faster if you can devote your full energy to its creation and marketing.

But without such luxury you will need a transition plan and the first step is to assess your situation. How much do you make at your job, for how many hours of work? Would you be allowed to pull out of your job gradually by going part time, or is it an all-or-nothing situation? Look at your personal requirements. How much money do you actually need to live on? Now take stock of your business. Based on the rates you charge or plan to charge, how many clients will it take on a regular basis to cover your financial needs? How many clients to fully replace your job income? Are you comfortable leaving your job once your business is making the bare minimum for you to get by on, or do you need it to replace your full job income?

When you have answers to these questions in hand, you are prepared to set transition benchmarks or milestones. You can set benchmarks in terms of money or number of clients. For example, say your goal is to replace your job salary of $30,000 per year, and that your boss says you can go part time to 20 hours when you're ready. This means that your first benchmark will be your business covering $15,000 gross yearly income, or $1,250 per month after business expenses. Decide how many months of hitting this mark you need to feel safe. For example, will you reduce your hours to 20 once you're averaging $1,250 over a three month period, or would six make you feel safer? Trainers, sitters, and boarders should be especially careful to take seasonal fluctuations into account in this decision.

To determine your monthly business income, subtract anything you spent on the business from the total you made for the month. Be sure to also subtract 1/12 of any yearly costs. For example, if you use your car for your business and spend an average of $1,500 per year on maintenance, your monthly car expense is $125—$1,500 divided by 12. And don't forget to factor in taxes and health insurance costs.

So once your business is consistently yielding $1,250 per month for the number of months you've required, request a reduction to 20 hours per week. Your second and final transition milestone is to put in your two weeks' notice when your business is consistently bringing in $2,500 per month after expenses. That way you know what you're shooting for, and you know when it's time to leave the job. No more guesswork or worrying.

A word on taxes

Don't forget to adjust your figures by 15% to account for self-employment taxes. For example, to replace $1,250 in work income a business would need to be making $1,437.50 per month, because 15% of $1,250 is $187.50. Consider discussing tax options with a qualified tax accountant—one who has had experience guiding small businesses of all entity types, including sole proprietorships, LLCs, and S Corporations. See Resources at the back of the book.

CASE STUDIES

Tracy had been transitioning into self-employment for a while, and the effects were taking their toll: dark circles under her eyes, a feeling of being over-whelmed, near-constant worry she'd forgotten something, and a growing strain on her relationship as her husband became increasingly resentful of the evenings and weekends she spent with her clients. But her old employer wasn't willing to let her work part time, and her training revenue could not yet cover her income. She needed a plan to get her through to the other side, and together we devised a clear schedule and marketing plan. She then explained her goals and plans to her husband who, relieved to see a light at the end of the tunnel, agreed to bear down and support her through it. She launched her marketing plan and, six months later, hit her milestone—for three months the business had made the same amount of income as her job. She gave notice and used the new time to reconnect with her husband and implement the larger of her marketing projects. She greatly enjoys working for herself and the reputation she has built as the go-to trainer in the area for serious behavior issues.

In contrast, Donna's transition was fast. Having taught classes for a large pet store chain for several years, she was aching to start her own business offering classes and private training out of her large converted garage. After we crunched the numbers to check the feasibility of starting her own training business, it was clear that a very modest number of clients would replace the income she was making at her job, and an assessment of her savings suggested that she could get up to that baseline while living on what she'd put away. Once we designed her business and marketing plan, Donna quit her job and launched her new venture. Her income now comfortably exceeds that from her previous job and she loves training on her own.

Paul's training business had grown as far as it could while he continued to work full time. It had been a slow, organic process based on word of mouth, just a couple clients a week and two weekend classes, but now he was ready to finally take a step toward his dream of training full time. He executed the first two projects of a thoroughly designed marketing plan, and the phone began ringing more often. Once he hit his benchmark number of clients per week he took the leap and scaled his job back to 20 hours to accommodate the new client load and additional time for marketing. Six months later he'd hit his ultimate milestone—the client load goal that indicated it was time to quit his job altogether. Nervous but excited, Paul gave notice and launched the next phase of his marketing plan. He now runs a well-regarded and successful training business.

Managing the transition

Managing the transition to becoming a full-time business owner takes forethought and perseverance. Sometimes everything goes perfectly, but usually there is a period of time where you're juggling more than feels comfortable.

For one thing, you likely only have limited outside financial support options, which means that your business will have to cover whatever your financial needs might be—whether that's replacing a previous job's income or reaching a bare minimum number for you to live on. You may have to take a cut in income and lifestyle for a while. It also means you may have some amount of time where you are working full time for a paycheck and devoting your free time to your business—both to handle clients and do your development and marketing. The longer you stay in this transition period, the less likely you are to make it to the other side—it simply gets exhausting, and when you are tired it's easy to become discouraged.

Here are some tips for managing your transition:

Stay focused. Keep the big picture in front of you. At the end of a long day when you're working a job, taking care of yourself and possibly a family, and trying to start your business, questions like "Why am I doing this?" can ring in your ears. Have the answer ready—that you're doing this to improve your quality of life, and when you reach the other side of the transition you'll be doing something you love for a living, and doing it on your own terms. Find whatever motivates you, and make it your mantra. Chant it to yourself whenever you begin to doubt your direction.

Make sacrifices consciously. If you are going to start a business while working, something will have to give. You probably can't do everything you already do and add this large project on top. Make conscious decisions at the outset about what you are willing to temporarily give up to make room for the business. If you don't make this decision it will be made for you, and you may be dismayed at what falls by the wayside—time for family and friends, exercise and mental health, and your own dog are the usual victims. Choosing what to set aside during your transition helps avoid such unintended consequences, and gives you a sense of being in control.

Set and schedule specific goals. Starting a business involves many decisions and tasks that will keep you very busy during the transition period. Without specific goals set out on a timeline, it's much easier to let certain tasks slip, keeping you in transition longer than necessary. Don't fall into this trap. Set goals for each month, and each week (especially for marketing!) and then place those goals into a schedule. Literally decide which blocks of time you will use to accomplish which tasks. If you know you will have two hours on Monday night and two on Wednesday and four hours on Saturday, decide in advance exactly what you will work on during each of those times. This will help you to use the limited time you have as effectively as possible.

Take good care of yourself. Transition can be a stressful and demanding time. Make sure you leave solid chunks of time in your schedule for personal activities that relax and stimulate you. You're much less likely to burn out before you reach your goals if you're feeling physically and mentally your best.

Ask for help. This is the time to rely on friends and family. Get them involved in this exciting phase of your business by asking them for help with specific tasks, or by asking them to take up slack in other areas while you focus on the business. Perhaps they can lend support with babysitting or food sharing or errands. Also consider seeking professional help with your transition. A business support coach or mentor can provide guidance and help you to move through this period as quickly as possible. For more ideas, see the Resources at the back of this book.

There's never a good time to be inefficient and disorganized

Yes, if you have five dog walking clients or teach just one puppy class a week, you can probably get away without being all that streamlined in your operations. But the moment you begin to grow and attract more clients, you'll encounter problems trying to keep up with that growth. At some point in time, nearly all businesses find themselves operating with systems designed for a smaller workload. In other words, what used to work for you no longer does. That's only natural as most of us prefer to concentrate on what we love—working with dogs—rather than updating our systems. But a good, hard look at your systems and how you operate, followed by the appropriate changes, is a cornerstone of business success.

So, when you find yourself in this position, it's time to pause and recreate, otherwise you continue to sacrifice efficiency and suffer needless stress. Recall Adam from Chapter 2 whose dog walking business was taking him for a walk. Taking clients from various parts of town and allowing them different numbers of days per week worked all right in the beginning, but once his business picked up, working that way was no longer feasible. Adam had to rethink his client strategy, and then put changes into place. If you find your business hindered by inefficiencies, you too should stop and reassess.

Start by clearly identifying the problem. What exactly is causing you to feel harried or stressed? What is causing the inefficiency? Now imagine what things would look like ideally. Adam, for example, wanted to minimize driving time, phone time, and pack management difficulties. Adam wanted his walkers to be able to pick up dogs within a single neighborhood. He wanted to stop the dozens of daily phone calls about whether a particular dog would or would not be walking the next day, and he wanted his walkers to walk the same dogs everyday so they could gel as a group. The next step was to devise a game plan for implementing these changes. For Adam this meant drafting new policies (in his case, full-time five-day-per-week clients only and no refunds for cancellations), discussing them with his walkers, and writing a letter to his clients. He set a deadline by which the changes would be made and a deadline by which clients had to notify him if they would no longer be using his services. Once he knew who was staying on board he assigned dogs to walkers based on geography and pack management guidelines (temperament, age, size, etc.). Any clients being assigned a different walker were introduced to the new service provider, walkers took newly assigned dogs out for practice runs, keys were reassigned, and by the deadline everyone was walking packs designed for efficiency.

This process took some additional effort and time, but once implemented made everyone's lives easier—especially Adam's. When you feel overwhelmed, the idea of stopping to take stock and then pursue a fix-it project seems impossible, but you must. The worst thing you can do is to keep running. Problems rarely fix themselves. In very extreme cases I've had clients actually close their businesses for a short period (for example, not schedule any clients for a week) in order to create the space needed to carry out an adjustment. If you can't imagine how to fix a problem or carry out a change, get some assistance. Though it's sometimes hard to see a solution when you're in the middle of a crisis, one nearly always exists.

When to expand and when to stay put

Expansion seems like an obvious goal for most business owners, but it is not always the best decision for everyone. Before you turn your successful private training business into a training center, or a thriving pet sitting business into a daycare, or hire walkers to take out additional packs, think it over carefully. Do you really want this new type of business? I ask the question because if you enjoy what you're doing now it would be a shame to move on to something you don't. Owning a business that exists in real space and has set office hours and overhead costs is not the same thing as owning a relatively simple home-based operation. Having pet sitting employees is not the same as being a pet sitter. So take a moment to really think through what a day in your new life would be like. Ask others who are doing it for some insight—how do they spend an average day? What do they most like? What do they most dislike? What has been most surprising?

And don't be afraid to scale back if your expansion doesn't suit you. If you feel you would enjoy a simpler life again, either hire someone to run the business (or aspects of it that you find challenging or burdensome), sell off part of your business if appropriate, or just scale back what you offer. A central purpose of owning a business, after all, is to better enjoy life.

CASE STUDY

After his first year in business, John's two walking packs were full but he continued to receive calls from potential clients. At first he explained he was fully booked and simply took down contact information in case of an opening. But it seemed a shame to turn away business, so John hired a walker and, once this person's pack was full, hired another. Soon he had three walkers working for him. At first he reveled in his success, but it didn't take long before he realized he was no longer enjoying his business. The stress of the additional paperwork, scheduling, and responsibility of looking after employees—especially when someone called in sick and his or her walks had to be covered—ultimately didn't feel worth the extra money. John considered his options and decided to go back to what had worked. He sold the extra clients to one of his employees and now John enjoys his own two walks a day—again.

Plan ahead

If you decide you would like to expand, have a plan before you begin. First, research the costs involved, both one-time up front costs (such as building a space or expanding the use of one you already have) and the ongoing monthly costs. A good real estate agent who handles commercial leases can help you figure space costs if that is part of your plan. Also determine the expense of contractors, your own labor, employees, marketing, and ongoing materials (such as office supplies, training supplies, food and toys, and whatever else you may need). Project your income based on the rates you will charge and a reasonable number of clients. It's a good rule of thumb to inflate costs and be modest about revenue—this creates a safe margin for error. In other words, go with the high end of your cost estimates and the low end of your revenue projections.

Compare these numbers to your current income and savings. Will you have enough money to proceed yourself, or will you need to borrow? If you need financial assistance, the next step is to research your options. Small business loan? Investors? Help from friends or family? Wait until you've saved enough?

Another decision is whether to expand all at once or in steps. Say you want to open a comprehensive dog services facility. One option is to go for it—open a large facility that offers a variety of services and has a full staff. The main advantage to this approach is in the marketing—you are able to tout yourself as a one-stop shop from the beginning. It may also afford you the opportunity to corner a market, if there's one available, and it provides multiple income streams. Another approach, which is financially less risky, is to determine which services will be most lucrative and begin with those on a smaller scale, with a plan to expand step by step as revenue allows. In this scenario, the initial offerings raise funds to add or widen a service, which then brings in additional resources to further develop the business, and so on. This could mean leasing a building but only utilizing part of it, or leasing a small building and moving to a larger one as needed. Buying is also an option, but unless you have a surplus of money and the real estate market is just right for it, it's often advisable to start your business life as a renter. Simply put, you're better able to choose the exact right space for your purpose after you've run your business for a number of months or years.

A full-scale business expansion is a complicated endeavor, the details of which are unique to each person's situation and geography, and so cannot be fully sketched out here. If you are contemplating launching such a project, you might benefit from professional support and guidance to help you reach your goals. Visit the Resources at the back of this book.

CASE STUDY

The daycare was nearing Tanisha's full capacity goal. It had been an exciting first year and a half, and Tanisha was proud of herself for starting her business without going into debt. Her next goal was to add boarding. She had the physical space for it in her facility, which is housed in a large warehouse, but it required new construction and the cost to cover it meant taking a loan. Because Tanisha was uncomfortable with that prospect, we devised a gradual expansion plan. Once she hit full daycare capacity, she took some net revenue and used it to build space for boarding two dogs. With the new revenue from the two boarding spaces she built a third space, and so on, until she had her boarding space fully developed. Her next plan is to add a training room using income from boarding.

Employees, independent contractors, and partners

One sure sign of success is the moment you realize you can no longer carry the work load on your own. If you make the decision to expand, you will need more bodies. Bringing in additional help allows you to grow your business, not only because you can accommodate an increased clientele, but more importantly because it provides you the ability to delegate. And that means more time to focus on what you do best, and more time to devote to growing, marketing, and nurturing your business. You have a number of options—hiring employees, hiring independent contractors, and bringing in a partner are most common—and choosing which path to take is a critical decision with many potential consequences.

Employees

The central advantage of using employees as a means of expansion is control. Unlike independent contractors and partners, you can tell an employee what to do and exactly how to do it. The downside is, of course, that it also increases your paperwork, adds the time and potential stress of management responsibilities, and creates additional expense.

Simply put, an employee is someone hired to work at a company. That person is paid an hourly wage or salary depending on the position, and the employer pays payroll taxes on the money paid to the employee, carries worker's compensation insurance, and must comply with federal and state workplace standards. The employer has full control over the employee—how she does her job, where and when she performs it, what materials she uses, etc. Employers may or may not offer health and other benefits.

Be prepared to spend time training your employees. While it is easy to tell someone what to do, it's important that they know exactly how you want them to do it. Better yet, involve employees in brainstorming and decision making to encourage a higher level of initiative. Good coaching and motivational skills are key to being a good employer and getting the most from your workers. Building a respectful, fun workplace is paramount, and doing so builds loyalty, which may lower your turnover rate. See the next chapter for more ideas on staff training and review.

But beware of the additional costs and hassles of being an employer. There is a significant amount of paperwork and cost involved in complying with governmental, labor, and payroll requirements. Becoming an employer is a big step to take and before you make the leap you should calculate all the costs—monetary and time—and compare them to the potential increase in revenue.

Independent contractors

One alternative to hiring employees is to utilize independent contractors. Properly used, an independent contractor can bring most of the benefits that an employee does but with far less hassle and cost. This is an often-misunderstood topic, so first, let's define what an independent contractor is.

An independent contractor (IC) is a person who owns his or her own business and contracts out time and services to another business. An independent contractor does not work for one employer only—he may contract himself out to multiple employers, and may also offer his own services directly to the public. An IC pays his own employment taxes and is responsible for his own insurance and medical coverage. You must, however, supply all independent contractors you paid more than $600 in a tax year with a 1099 form reporting whatever you paid them for their services. This is a relatively simple procedure, and your tax accountant or the IRS can provide you assistance if necessary.

An IC schedules his own time and uses his own materials to carry out his work. Of course, if a contract calls for an IC to teach a public class at a certain time, for example, he has to teach it at that time. But he agreed to that, rather than it being dictated to him. An IC is not trained by the people who hire him.

I often hear dog pros talk about hiring subcontractors when, really, they are referring to independent contractors. A subcontractor is someone hired by an IC. A common example is when a building contractor is hired by someone to build a structure. That contractor will most likely turn around and hire an electrician and a plumber to carry out installation of those building features. The electrician and plumber would be subcontractors. You don't see much subcontracting in the dog services industry.

Generally it is to your financial advantage to hire independent contractors if you can. Hiring employees is much more expensive—you have the payroll taxes, worker's compensation insurance, and a whole host of other costs. There is also a lot of paperwork involved, and the implications of not doing these things properly can be disastrous. The IRS and other federal and state agencies, including your state's unemployment compensation insurance agency and worker's compensation insurance agency, do not look kindly upon mistakes or unfiled documentation.

It looks like a clear-cut case for hiring independent contractors, right? But unfortunately the IRS and other federal and state agencies don't much like it when businesses do that. The IRS and state tax departments dislike the use of ICs because they don't receive the same level of taxes and because it can be easier to hide income as an IC. The federal and state labor agencies don't like IC arrangements because they aren't able to easily control workplace treatment and protection for ICs. Consequently these agencies place a lot of rules on the hiring of independent contractors. If you hire an IC who the IRS or another agency thinks should have been classified as an employee, you can face audits, back taxes with interest tacked on, and large fines.

The main rules of thumb for hiring an independent contractor are that she:

- owns her own business
- is generally able to choose where to do her work
- also makes her services directly available to the public
- can only be let go based on the terms of the IC agreement
- uses her own materials and supplies
- is paid a flat rate for a project, rather than by the hour
- has multiple clients
- works on a finite project rather than working for you over a long period of time
- can determine how best to go about her work, rather than heeding your instructions
- is not trained by you
- sets her own work hours
- provides services that are not central to the day-to-day operation of your business
- has the professional skills necessary to carry out the tasks she is hired for
- does not receive workplace benefits
- pays her own taxes

You may be worrying at this point—these rules are hard to follow. Some people point to precedent, though you cannot rely in total on it. Because it is common precedent in our industry to hire independent contractors for many things, such as teaching public classes, pet sitting, and dog walking, there is a line of thought that we are all protected in doing so. That's simply not true. Precedent may help your case, but you should know that it does not make it a slam dunk, and our industry is seeing more and more cases of dog pros brought to task by the IRS over misclassification of ICs.

There are some excellent resources at the back of this book to provide additional help in making decisions about whether to hire independent contractors or employees and, once you've chosen, to help you carry out your decision. The risk that someone will challenge your hiring of ICs over employees is relatively low. The IRS or another agency might take a look at your classification of workers if, by chance, you were flagged for an IRS audit, or if someone filed a complaint against you with a state or federal agency. Still, weigh the decision carefully—a problem in this area can be financially devastating.

Bringing in a partner

Another way to grow your business is by bringing in a business partner. This can be an excellent way to get help without the issues involved with employees or independent contractors. With a partner, you can truly share the load. You get someone who is personally invested in seeing the business succeed, which means you are likely to get someone's best and most focused work. A good partner will also do whatever it takes, rather than knocking off when work hours are over. The disadvantages are that you may have to give up 100% control of your ship, and if you are temperamentally unsuited to each other or begin to disagree on major points of direction, things can get very difficult. But with the right person, two can definitely be more than the sum of their parts, and sharing the responsibility, joys, and disappointments can be a great relief and make the work that much more fun, too.

Of course, if you decide to bring in a partner, even if you're married to them or have been best friends since diapers, put everything in writing. Even if you don't run into conflicts, having your business plan detail who is responsible for what, and having a process for how decisions are made and profits shared, all in writing, makes for a smoother sailing ship.

CASE STUDY

Patricia knew it was time to get some help. Now that her business was doing so well she just couldn't keep up with all the tasks involved in operating and marketing it while still taking good care of clients, too. She considered hiring help, but wasn't sure she wanted the responsibility of looking after an employee. She shared her ruminations with Suzie, a close friend from college, and it turned out that her friend was considering moving back to the area but hadn't found work yet. What's more, she had a degree in business and loved dogs. They decided to team up, and Suzie joined the business as a partner. Now Patricia works with clients and Suzie runs the business, and as a result, the business has taken off and Patricia enjoys being freed from the bulk of the business tasks while also enjoying the camaraderie of a shared endeavor.

Teaming up with another business

Another creative solution for growth is to team up either officially or in a loose affiliation with another business. For example, you might join forces with another dog pro based on complementary services. Perhaps you do private training and often get calls for public classes. Maybe another trainer in the area teaches classes but doesn't offer privates. You could each expand your services, or you could band together to share clients. Whether you actually legally combine the businesses or simply share some common expenses and tasks, you will both benefit. You can, for example, share marketing expenses and efforts. You could centralize scheduling and supply orders. If you find someone with complementary skills—say one of you is great at marketing and the other at organizing—you may be able to cut each person's workloads and more effectively play to each of your strengths.

CASE STUDIES

Monica met Dana, another pet sitter, at a dinner party thrown by a mutual friend. They shared stories of the hassles and expense of trying to market their businesses. They also talked about difficult clients they'd had and traded their best animal war stories. At the end of the evening they agreed it had felt great to talk to someone else who understood what it was like to be an independent pet sitter. At home later that night Monica was struck with an idea. She called Dana the next day and, over coffee, they outlined a plan for a loose coalition of pet sitters that would pool resources for marketing and meet regularly for support and good company. Over time they've found that the larger scale marketing they can afford as a group has brought them all an increase in their client base, and that the monthly meetings have been a great source of ideas, support, and collegiality.

Sonja and Tammy were both excellent public class instructors. Sonja taught primarily puppy and obedience based classes, whereas Tammy focused on agility and specialized classes such as Canine Good Citizen and tricks. Old friends from training school, they often commiserated over the difficulty of finding and keeping class spaces, and the time and money spent on marketing. It finally occurred to them to team up. Combining their resources enabled them to lease a dedicated space and get more marketing value for their money and efforts. And because one's class content complemented the other's so well, clients had many choices to bring them back after the first class.

Interns and assistants

Offering paid or even unpaid internships or assistant positions can also take pressure off. People are often happy to trade their time for experience, education, or sometimes even just time with dogs. It is common for group class instructors and daycares to have assistants, for example. Some assistants help out as a hobby and a way to be around dogs, but many give their time because they want to learn dog training or the daycare ropes. Creating a strong, supportive atmosphere may lead some of these people to eventually become ICs or employees. Trainers can also use assistants or interns in their private practices, particularly as handlers when working with dog or human aggression issues. Again, the helper gains experience and knowledge from the mentoring trainer. Dog walkers and pet sitters might also consider such an approach for short-term relief. The obvious advantage is free labor; the disadvantage a high turnover in many cases. Still, it can be a good stop-gap measure. To make the most of this approach and its advantages, create a dedicated program with an application process, clear expectations and goals on both sides, and a structured use of time.

Don't wait too long to hire

Whatever form of help you decide to seek, don't wait too long. Most dog service businesses are one-person affairs. If you run one, you know what it's like to juggle a multitude of tasks and wear too many hats at once: trainer/walker/sitter/daycare or boarding operator, plus administrative assistant, marketing manager, bookkeeper, account-ant, customer service rep, even janitor.

I find in our business consulting work and when on the road speak-ing at conferences and seminars that many dog pros are exhausted by the pressure of keeping up—or the stress of not being able to. When I suggest hiring some help, the reaction is often shock. "Oh, I couldn't do that. I can't afford it." The question is, "Can you afford not to?"

You can afford it, really

You may not be in a position to bring on a full-time salaried employee, but that's not your only option. Start small if you must. Even hiring someone for five hours a week can take a good deal of pressure off. It's not just the five hours of work another person can get done for you—it's also the peace of mind of having those particular tasks ticked off your list.

And don't forget the five hours you suddenly have that didn't exist before. Five hours a week to build your business and make more money. Say you hire an admin assistant to help five or ten hours a week with answering emails and returning phone calls. Right away you're improving business by improving your response time to poten-tial clients. Or maybe you'd like assistance with your bookkeeping or other paperwork, perhaps some cleaning around your facility if you have one. Now you have five or ten hours to work on marketing or to add client screening appointment times or an extra dog walk or pet sit. Already the money you pay your assistant is paying dividends. And if you're really over-taxed, you might grab some of that extra time for yourself, too.

9

Building the Perfect Staff

You know you've arrived when you can take a vacation or leave for an unexpected family emergency and come back to find everything in order: a relaxed staff fully in control, a happy clientele, and well-behaved dogs. Though a little ego bruising, a good staff should make you feel redundant, at least where day-to-day operations are concerned. This leaves you free to pursue what you most enjoy, whether it be big picture thinking, creating new programs, working with the dogs, or taking more vacations.

But this kind of staff doesn't just happen—it's created, through careful hiring decisions, deliberate and ongoing training, and management via staff reviews. Without a plan for hiring, training, and managing staff, expanding can quickly become a nightmare in which having "help" actually makes more work for you. Taking the time to plan your hiring and training process up front, even when you've waited too long to hire and are in desperate need of help, makes it much more likely you'll actually get that help.

What would you like help with?
Before you hire, decide what kind of assistance would be most helpful. Does the admin side of your business bog you down? Then consider hiring administrative help to allow you more time to market or add sitting appointments. But sometimes it's the direct service duties, like running the daycare floor or walking the boarding dogs, that keep you from other pressing tasks. If you feel you don't have time to run the business side of your operation it might be more helpful to hire someone to care for the dogs. Hiring a daycare floor

attendant, for example, allows you to spend some time in the office returning phone calls, handling paperwork, and taking care of marketing—which helps your business to grow.

Which kind of position to hire for is a personal decision, and I advise making it that way—what do you personally want to do less of? What would you like more time for? One of the reasons you went into business for yourself was to enjoy life more, to be your own boss, to be in charge of your day and how you spend your time. So hire accordingly to release yourself from tasks that make you dread your day, weigh you down, or cause you stress.

What to look for

Once you've decided what you want help with, make a list of the specific tasks you want that person to accomplish for you. Then write down the skills and qualities needed to tackle these successfully. This second list is what you're looking for in your new hire. Keep in mind when considering candidates that some skills are easier to acquire than others. For example, if the person you bring on will be interacting with existing and potential clients, prioritize customer service and language skills over dog knowledge. It's much easier to train someone to interact with dogs than retrain how they behave with humans.

Don't underestimate the importance of a strong personality match. You'll have to be around this person on a regular basis. And if you have employees, they will, too. In addition to whatever skills and qualities you seek, look for a team player. Nothing sours a workplace faster than someone who is negative or unable to get along with others.

Who to hire, and where to find them

Start by looking around you. Is there someone you know who might fit the bill? Consider acquaintances, including your clients. I've often seen particularly strong training class students become excellent training assistants, for example. Or maybe there's a client you find intelligent and articulate who's looking for some extra work. And if not, maybe she knows someone who is. You won't know if you don't ask.

If putting the word out informally within your personal network fails, broaden your search. Put together a job announcement and post it to the places that make the most sense in your area. Online avenues like craigslist.org can be a good bet. If you live in a college town, post to the job boards there to find a responsible grad student. This is also a good time to use government unemployment listing resources, as so many qualified and talented people are looking for work.

Writing an effective job description

The type of candidates you see will depend in part on your job posting. If you want serious, qualified, committed folks to apply but are only hearing from sixteen-year-olds who mumble and avoid eye contact, it's time to rework your post. Look at job postings for serious positions and model yours on them.

Your description should include a bulleted list of the responsibilities involved, and another of the skills and qualities you are looking for in a candidate. Make some reference to higher education as well. Depending on your area you may either require a college degree or mention a preference for one. By so doing you signal that you are looking for a mature, accomplished adult. Finally, require that all interested parties apply with a cover letter and resume. Requiring a formal application helps to weed out less serious and skilled applicants, and saves you time lost to drop-ins and phone calls.

Interview to separate the wheat from the chaff

Interviewing potential hires is a much more complicated process than it seems. It's all too easy to get through a lengthy interview process and learn nothing of real value to help with our decision making. For one thing, we're very good at telegraphing to others what we want to hear. And for another, we rarely ask the kinds of questions or put people in the kinds of situations that would give us any insight into how they might be on the job.

Here are some tips for effective interviewing:
Refer back to the lists you made

You decided what you want your new employee to be able to do, and what skills they need. The interview process should be built around these lists or it won't serve you as it should.

Don't tell candidates what you're looking for

If you tell a potential hire you're looking for a team player who takes initiative, she's going to tell you (if she has any smarts at all) that she's that person. Instead, ask questions and listen to her answers, and to the questions she asks in return.

Ask application-based questions

Want to know if someone is a team player? Asking outright will telegraph what you're hoping to hear. Instead, present the candidate with a scenario and ask her what she'd do. For example, "Let's say you notice something that isn't being done as well as you think it could be. What would you do?" Or if you want to know if her default response to dogs is positive or negative you might ask, "How would you handle a dog who is barking excessively?"

Put candidates in real-life situations

If you want to see how a potential hire might handle a difficult client and/or test her writing skills, give her a sample client email and ask her to write a response. If you want to gauge her comfort around dogs, put her on the daycare floor. Can she read body language? Ask her to watch two rambunctious players and tell you when she'd step in to ask them to take a short break. And getting back to her cooperation skills, you might also ask her to engage in a task with you or another employee to see how she handles a group project.

Keeping the good ones

Once you have a hire you're happy with, do everything you can to keep her happy, too. It's worth the effort not to have to repeat the hiring process again. Take the time, regularly, to let your hire know what you appreciate about her and her work. A little praise goes a long way and, just like we do with dogs, we humans sometimes forget to let each other know when we've done a good job.

Be flexible where you can be about schedules, particularly if you're unable to offer a full-time position just yet. Keep the job interesting by adding new responsibilities or projects, particularly for employees who enjoy being creative, learning new things, or being relied on. And openly welcoming suggestions and ideas from your staff keeps everyone feeling engaged and a valued part of a team.

But perhaps the best way to keep employees happy—and keep yourself happy with them—is to engage in effective staff training and a productive evaluation process.

Staff training

Job training is essential to the success of your business. The better trained your employees are, the smarter they work. Well-trained employees are more engaged and more likely to solve problems independently. Because they feel more valued, they are happier in their jobs, which in turn is reflected in their productivity.

And yet, job training is often random and uninspired. An outgoing employee shows a new person the ropes in whichever way he or she likes. A manager spends half an hour going over a new piece of equipment. One complaint too many triggers a lecture-style presentation by the owner on "best practices" in customer service. But job training should be forward-looking, interactive, and carefully planned—it should be an integral part of your business strategy, not something you are forced into by circumstances.

Train with purpose

Base your job-training program on your job descriptions. What do you want your employees to know and what do you want them to do? Your program should teach and develop that knowledge and those skills. The more clarity and precision your job descriptions have, the easier it is to design a staff-training program.

Design for the long haul. Training should be ongoing, not reserved for new employees or left until problems arise. You can follow this strategy and still allow for tactical, one-off sessions to address specific problems or to teach new skills. (Don't be afraid to ask employees for ideas about topics for ongoing training. People on the front lines are often the ones with the greatest insights into what might improve everyday work life for staff and the service experience for customers.)

Set goals

A training topic—or fancy title—doth not a training session make. In other words, don't mistake a training topic for the intended outcome of the session. Customer service may be the topic and *How to Wow* the title, but for training to be successful you need a clear set of goals for your desired outcome.

Goals should be:

Specific. Spell out what you want people to know and do. "This training will be about customer service" is a non-descriptive statement about a topic broad enough to encompass most anything.

115

By contrast, "Learning protocols for greeting clients in the morning rush" describes the content of the training session in specifics. "Learning to read canine body language" is too broad; "Recognizing when a dog is anxious" is well defined.

Measurable. Another problem with broad goals like "Learning to give good customer service" is that they are tough to measure. What would the yardstick be? No more client complaints ever? A measurable goal would be "Employee will be able to follow phone protocol." The goal "Take good care of the dogs" is open to interpretation, whereas "Keeping kennels clean" or "Using positive feedback whenever a dog greets you calmly and politely" is immediately quantifiable.

Achievable. "Learning basic training skills" is a specific and measurable goal, but it is too big a project to achieve to any satisfying level in just one training session. Instead, aim for something like "Learn basic luring techniques and when to reward."

Make the time

Though many business owners believe in and plan for staff training and skill development ("I fully intend to do that some day!"), few actually find the time to do anything about it. Training is left until a crisis hits and circumstances force the situation. To make staff training a reality, first of all prioritize it. Think of it as a regular, ongoing business task that has to be worked into the schedule for, say, every third Thursday. Second of all, make it mandatory. Anything else undermines the importance of the program. And third, keep sessions short. Resist the temptation to do too much in one sitting—with training sessions happening regularly, there is no need.

The more content you squeeze in, the less attendees will retain. Pick one thing and focus on it.

Make training effective and fun

One of the biggest training sins employers commit is to choose a lecture format for their training program. The research is unequivocal on this. People retain only about ten percent of what is said in a lecture, making it a very poor way to teach anybody anything.

Instead, make your training interactive. Provide plenty of opportunities for your employees to apply the ideas in practice. In addition to increasing the likelihood that the learning will stick, this approach has the further benefit of giving you the chance to see what they are learning.

Step 1. Get people invested by asking them to participate from the very beginning.

- Send out a survey before the training, for example, asking people to contribute their experiences, concerns, questions, thoughts, etc. about the upcoming topic. In each case consider whether the survey should be anonymous, and whether it will be optional or mandatory.

- Request a case study. Giving people a form to fill out often makes this easier and yields better information. The form might include questions like: What happened? What did you do? What were the results? How did you feel about it? What questions did this experience raise that you would like to see addressed?

- Give people a short article to take a look at. Ask them to make notes for discussion.

And so on. The idea is to get people to interact with the material before the event. Say you were doing a training session on how to deal with difficult customers. You might send out an anonymous survey asking people to contribute a recent experience they found stressful and ask for details about how the scenario played out, the customer's reactions, the results, how the staff person felt about the experience, and what questions he or she was left with.

Step 2. Always open your training with an interactive opportunity.

- A brainstorming session, for example. Have people throw out ideas or questions or examples and write them all on a whiteboard for later discussion. (Always have a few examples up your sleeve to get the ball rolling if nobody volunteers.)

- A quick poll. Prepare questions ahead of time and have someone capture the figures for some on-the-spot statistics: 60% of Castor Kennel staff finds the cleaning manual confusing. Who knew?

Opening a training session this way gets people engaged and avoids setting the expectation that they are just going to sit and listen. Follow up by stating the goals of the session and, where possible, tying those goals into something your employees shared during the opening segment.

If we return to the hypothetical training session about difficult customers, you might open that by asking people to brainstorm the kinds of customer situations they find especially difficult.

Step 3. A lecture/presentation.

- Cover the points you want to make, and the things you want to teach.
- Keep it brief.
- Load it up with examples.

In the customer training example, you might use the presentation part of the session to outline strategies for how to defuse troublesome situations, provide specific language for employees to use when a customer has a complaint, and describe the complaint process from A to Z, so everyone knows what is required of them if and when a customer is unhappy.

Step 4. Give people a chance to apply what they have learned.

- Whatever format you choose, be careful not to put people on the spot. Begin by showing what you want people to do, while narrating what you are doing. Then give people a different scenario and ask them to brainstorm as a group how it might be tackled. If applicable, demonstrate their suggestions, and then ask everyone to chime in on how the proposed solution worked.
- If you ask people to carry out a task or role-play, don't make them do it in front of the whole group. Avoid anything that smacks of performance or testing; this is training. Instead, break people into groups or pairs, or give individual tasks that people can self-assess by comparing against an answer sheet. (Any performance-like role-playing should always be on a volunteer basis only.)

In our difficult customer training example, this step might be a scripted role-play between you and another manager or a confident, pre-recruited employee. The role-play would be followed by a discussion in which you ask the group to analyze what you did and why it worked.

Then, in a second role-play, things should go less smoothly. Your counterpart would now throw complications at you. Stop at various points during the role-play and ask your employees to give you specific advice about how to handle the situation. Again, ask for input about what works and why, and what alternative approaches one might consider.

Finally, you could have your employees role-play a new situation in pairs, letting them stop at various points to discuss how to handle things. (If an employee wants to role-play in front of everyone, take on the role of customer yourself. That way you can ensure the experience is useful, not painful, for your employee. Allow him or her to pause the action at any point and get suggestions from the whole group.)

Make it count

Training is too often carried out in a vacuum, unrelated to everyday routines and problems. Tie training topics to daily protocols, systems, etc., and follow up to make sure procedures are applied. Use daily or weekly checklists to make this easier. Say you do a staff training on proper phone protocol. Provide a form that guides people step by step through the protocol while they are on the phone. Or, if your staff training focused on proper opening and closing protocols, provide checklists for people to follow.

Remember to reinforce the behavior you want. Make a point of complimenting people when you see them applying what they have learned during a training session.

Finally, tie your staff training into performance reviews. When you go through the trouble and expense of providing training on a subject, you are entitled to hold people accountable for what they have learned. And yet most staff reviews bear no relation to day-to-day tasks, centering instead on vague, generic standards for dress code and attitude. When your job descriptions, staff training, and performance reviews are in sync, you are much more likely to have a smooth-running business where everybody knows their role and plays it competently.

Staff reviews

Staff performance reviews enjoy near-universal unpopularity—dreaded by employer and employee alike. For the employer, reviews feel like meaningless busywork, something you are expected to do that never really seems productive or useful. Many employers are also uncomfortable having to assess people and possibly deliver criticisms. For the employee, the process can be both punishing and embarrassing.

Some avoid reviews altogether. In another common scenario, the responsible manager downloads a generic HR template online that contains only superficial review criteria for things that have little meaning and no direct relevance to the company in question. Or, to avoid conflict, the manager reviews the employee more favorably than what he or she really deserves. Either way, it means that even when reviews happen they seldom have the impact they should, i.e., move the company and the individuals who comprise it forward.

The good news is, it doesn't have to be like this. The staff review process can be a useful tool for everyone involved, helping to build a smooth-running business that is enjoyable to own and work for.

Reviews that work

First, tie staff reviews to job descriptions and any staff training you do so the items under review are directly relevant. Make the items specific. For example, rather than reviewing an item called "Attitude," a concept too broad to be a useful starting point for a discussion, have an item called "Willingness to Help Colleagues and Go Above and Beyond Where Needed." A detailed item like this gives you specific instances to refer to when assessing how an employee measures up.

Second, make feedback meaningful. The format of review feedback is often an undefined scale, for example 1 to 10. Say we know 10 is excellent and 1 is bad. That still leaves us without a definition of what it takes to be a 10 or any shared understanding of the numbers in between. One employee might be proud of receiving an 8; another might see it as a rebuke. Neither knows what the 8 is meant to convey. Instead of vague scales, use rubrics.

A rubric is essentially a defined scale. Each number or rung on the scale is clearly spelled out.

How to use rubrics

Make the scale short. 1 to 4, for example, rather than 1 to 10. This makes the rubrics easier to write and use, and leaves less room for haggling, misinterpretations, and so on.

Be specific. People need to know exactly what you mean by a particular score and what is expected of them.

When writing rubrics, it is often helpful to start by creating a generic example. Something along the lines of:

4: Exhibits complete mastery.

3: Highly competent with some additional room for learning.

2: Basic skills and competencies in place.

1: Does not meet basic requirements.

Guided by this generic rubric, you are now ready to write rubrics for the individual employee's points of review. Say a point of review is "Recognizes Tension on the Daycare Floor and Acts Proactively to Defuse Unsafe Situations and Avoid Incidents." That would translate into the following rubric:

4: Consistently reads overt and subtle body language and reacts early with appropriate measures to keep dogs out of conflict.

3: Recognizes most body language and tensions, and responds in time to defuse tensions and avoid conflicts in most cases.

2: Able to read obvious body language signals and respond in time to avoid conflict in those cases.

1: Does not recognize enough body language to proactively respond to avoid conflict or may recognize body language but does not respond proactively.

Be prepared to share examples to back up your scores. Name specific incidents and observations. Say you give an employee a score of 2 on the above rubric because you have seen this person miss subtle signs of resource guarding, making him or her unable to respond as quickly as is ideal. If at all possible, share specific incidents, like "The tiff between Fido and Spot over the pink tennis ball."

Be as positive with feedback as possible. Don't focus exclusively on areas that need attention—give at least equal weight to things employees do well. And then be specific about areas for improvement, couching such suggestions in the context of the rubric. As in: "You are doing a great job noticing when chase and wrestle games are getting too heated and stepping in on those. What I'd like you to work on next to move from a 2 to a 3 is recognizing some of the more subtle signs dogs give each other when they feel possessive about a toy or another resource." Follow up with a specific plan for accomplishing this improvement. For example, is there a staff training you would like the person to attend? Is there a DVD to watch or a book to read? Will you pair him or her up with a colleague who has these skills?

Set goals on day one

Even the best employees cannot be expected to read minds. Don't make it a mystery how to be the model employee; nobody should be left to guess. Give new employees the review points (in rubric form) the day you hire them, so they know exactly what is expected of them and what to strive for.

Get employees involved

Self-assessment can be a powerful tool, worth incorporating into your review process. The potential gains:

1. Getting employees involved in the review process helps them better understand what they are being evaluated on and what you are looking for.

2. Employees who actively participate in the process are less likely to be taken aback by their scores, which means that conflict stemming from defensiveness and embarrassment is less likely.

3. If the rubrics are clear and well thought through, an employee's perspective on his or her job performance is less likely to be far off yours. And if it is, you will have a clear sense of any areas in which perspective is out of whack or where expectations have not been clearly communicated *before* you go into the one-on-one review.

Give the employee the review and ask him to complete it before his scheduled review appointment and bring it with him. At the review, go point by point, asking the employee to share his self-score and to explain why he has scored himself this way. If your score matches, give any additional thoughts or examples to reinforce his. If not, tell the employee what you agree with in his self-analysis and explain why you have scored him differently, again using examples and specific incidents wherever possible. Avoid any negotiation. Your score IS the score—unless you realize there is a compelling reason to do so, do not change your score. If the employee's score was higher than what you gave him, give specific examples and direction for how the score can be raised to the one the employee gave himself.

Be goal-oriented

In addition to going over the rubric review points, use your staff review appointment to set concrete goals for each employee between now and the next review. Keep the goals to a limited number—something in the region of two or four, depending on the complexity of goals and length of review period. Be sure to define what success will look like. How will you and your employee know if the goals were met?

> **A non-concrete goal:** Improve your understanding of dogs.

> **A concrete goal:** Improve reading of canine body language, specifically recognizing signs of resource guarding.

In this instance, success would be quantifiably fewer incidents/tiffs on the playground.

Create an action plan with benchmarks and interim deadlines to make sure the work required to achieve the goals is not left to a mad dash right before the next review. Having progress meetings along the way reignites motivation for getting things done, shows support of employees and their development, and helps you catch early on if things are not moving along as hoped.

The first time you institute this goal program, start with simpler goals on a shorter time frame. For example, if you carry out reviews twice a year, make the goals quarterly. This is another great place to get your employees involved. Have them fill out a goal sheet in which they suggest areas for their own improvement or professional development. Have some ideas of your own prepared and decide with your employees which goals they will pursue this quarter. Make sure at least one of them comes from their own list and is of strong interest to them.

From here on out, the review process is made up of assessing goal success, revisiting your rubrics for the position in question, and setting the next quarter's goals.

Everyone wins

A review process that includes collaborative goal setting and employee involvement is much less aversive and uncomfortable for both parties. It creates a greater sense of responsibility for one's own job performance. And it allows you to be an effective manager and leader, rather than merely The Boss.

And these techniques for training and reviewing staff mean it's much more likely you'll come back from your next vacation to find everything went swimmingly without you.

10

Feeling the Burn: Avoiding Professional Burnout

No business owner completely escapes burnout—it simply comes with the territory. However, there are strategies anyone can adopt to prevent the most common headaches and keep energized. The benefits of keeping a regular schedule and having realistic expectations are obvious, though no less important for that reason, whereas other potential trouble spots, like giving free advice and being too generous with yourself on the phone, rarely occur to people until there's a real problem. Considering such potential sore spots up front, the ones that will otherwise become raw and bothered, will save you a world of frustration down the road.

"How about Tuesday at 6?" What a master schedule can do for you

One pitfall of self-employment is the lack of a routine. If a flexible schedule without a boss and specific deadlines makes you feel rudderless, working for yourself can be a challenge. It's easy to do little or nothing when you have unlimited time. I've seen dog pros struggle for months to do what could have been done in weeks or even days. To keep yourself working toward your goals without losing focus, make a realistic schedule and commit to deadlines. Avoid losing time by structuring your workdays carefully. What days will you see clients? When will you work on training plans? When will you take care of administrative tasks? When will you spend time growing your business?

It's easy to see how tending to your business can fall through the cracks when you add together life responsibilities such as family and the inevitable appointments with doctors and auto mechanics along with personal goals like exercise, spending time with friends and one's own dogs—not to mention just trying to enjoy some free time. A good schedule can help you manage your work and personal responsibilities as efficiently as possible, which in turn will allow you more time for personal goals. And a schedule can relieve anxiety by eliminating the need to worry about what you're forgetting or fret about things not getting done.

There are many ways to approach building a master schedule, and it's important to pick a style that matches your temperament. Here are two formats to consider.

The guideline schedule

A guideline schedule is a good choice if you're looking for plenty of flexibility and enjoy a high degree of self discipline. In this schedule you assign days or blocks of time to various possible tasks. For example, you might relegate weekday afternoons to paperwork, down time, or errands. You then can decide each week or each day how to spend your time, based on your own desires and what needs to be done.

The detailed schedule

If you have a procrastinator's tendencies, often feel disorganized, and know that you need structure to thrive, the detailed schedule can help you run your business smoothly. This schedule assigns days and blocks of time to each task and is followed in the same format each week. It provides a rhythm and order that ensures a place for everything, and removes the daily worry over how best to spend time, and the guilt over not spending it the way you think you should. With this schedule, work time is clearly defined, and when it's time for play you need not feel guilty.

Lumping versus splitting

Dog trainers, thanks to Bob Bailey, often talk about lumping versus splitting when making criteria decisions. I like to apply this concept to scheduling. It's a work style choice: do you prefer to focus on one thing for an extended period of time, or do you feel more comfortable frequently shifting tasks? Would you rather do your business paperwork in one fell swoop? Then assign it to one day a week and clear as much else away from that day as possible. For example, a trainer might get up and walk the dog or exercise in the morning, lump administrative work from 11 to 4, then prep for evening clients and have dinner before leaving for the evening training sessions.

Generally speaking, it is more efficient to work this way, as you lose time with each transition from one task to another. But if focusing on one thing for long periods of time is not your work style, or the nature of your business doesn't allow for it, or you have unsavory tasks you can't face in large doses, you can split things into smaller portions. A dog walker who is home from walking late each afternoon could assign herself administrative work in two smaller sessions on Tuesday and Thursday after walking.

How to build your master schedule

Start with a fresh piece of paper and mark off the days of the week, without any actual dates (or use a computer calendar program). If working on paper use a pencil. You can also have several sheets in order to try multiple approaches and be able to compare them side by side.

On another sheet make a list of all your tasks and obligations, and all the other things you want time for. Organize the list into categories—one for your business, one for any other work obligations you might have, and one for your personal and home life. You can break the categories down into smaller pieces if that's helpful to you.

Plug in tasks or commitments with set times first. For example, if you go to yoga classes twice a week, put them down—they're the same time every week and you can't change them.

Next consider any items that have general time constraints. For example, if you will be teaching classes, you know that they're generally taught Monday through Thursday evenings and Saturday/Sunday daytimes. Dogs have to be walked Monday through Friday daytimes.

Look at the remaining items and the openings on your schedule. Think about your own work patterns and daily rhythms. For example, are you most alert and focused in the morning? Perhaps one or more morning slots would be best for business paperwork. Do you find yourself a little sleepy in the afternoon? This would be a good time to schedule in the daily walk with your own dogs.

Don't forget other peoples' schedules, too. If seeing friends more often is a priority, be sure to consider their work schedules.

And remember to give yourself days off. Too many dog professionals report enjoying only occasional days away from work, rarely two in a row, and that a regular weekend seems an impossibility. But I've found in working with our clients that regular weekly time off is absolutely achievable with a well-formulated schedule. And not prioritizing downtime is a quick path to burnout.

Protect your schedule
Your schedule will only work for you if you protect it. If you've built in a set time for facility tours, don't be pressed into giving them outside those hours. Avoid the temptation to work during your downtimes. And don't schedule appointments that aren't in your master schedule. If you've offered a potential client all your available slots for next week and they respond that none work, give them your slots for the week after. If those don't work either, or they insist on a day on which you don't see clients, simply tell them, kindly but confidently, "I'm so sorry. I don't have appointments on Mondays. It looks like I may not be able to accommodate you. I could give you a referral to a colleague who may have better availability if none of my spots can work for you." You'll be surprised to find that nearly all people—I'd go so far as to say nine of ten—will suddenly find that perhaps one of your spots could work after all. Though everyone likes to be catered to, people respond to confidence and like the idea of working with someone so successful they don't need to chase every lead.

Set boundaries for the phone and email
This is a tough issue for small dog service businesses. We all know the scenario—you return a message that is an hour old and hear, "Oh, thanks, but I've already found someone." One or two of these experiences is all it takes for many dog pro business owners to check email obsessively and to frantically reach for the phone at the first ring, at any hour of day or night, weekday or weekend. And, of course, to carry that smart phone everywhere, rushing out of restaurants and movies when it vibrates, or interrupting a good conversation to return an email.

It's a quandary. If you let the phone rule you, you become tired and burned out from constantly being on call. You also teach your clients to expect your availability at all times, thus perpetuating the evil cycle. On the other hand, no one wants to lose potential clients. What to do?

I strongly urge having off hours—hours that your business is closed and the ringer and computer are turned off. You might lose a few clients, but you are likely to enjoy your work much more and stay in business for the long haul. A few clients now are not worth an early career change.

There are also ways to lessen the negative effect of time away from your smart phone. When you choose your set phone hours, for example, try to include the most common times the phone rings so that you catch the majority of calls. Spend some time on your outgoing message and email auto reply—what people hear or see there can make a difference. Let them know you're out training or walking or caring for dogs on the daycare floor, and you look forward to giving them and their dog the same undivided attention. Tell them when to expect to hear from you. Giving the precise hours you return calls or emails each day is preferable to a broad timeframe such as "within 24 hours." Most potential clients will wait instead of moving on to another service provider if they feel confident they'll hear from you, and know when to expect to. You can up the ante here by recording your outgoing message and updating your autoreply each day. Leading with the date, "Thank you for calling Good Dog. Today is Tuesday the 18th... " lets people know yours is a well-run, professional business they'll certainly hear back from, and that there's no need to continue shopping.

Also think about getting help with your phone and email. Though you are probably the best at selling what you have to offer, the right person can be effective for you, and it's better than a message machine. When you're first starting out perhaps a friend or family member would be willing to pilot the phone for a couple hours a day. Once you're established and growing well you may choose to pay someone for this service, or to pay someone for other work to free yourself to answer the phone and sell your services.

Set clear expectations—for clients and of them

Clear expectations help to avoid conflict and frustration for both you and your clients. Setting them is both professional and a kindness.

See your clients as you see their dogs

One of the things I love about positive reinforcement dog training is the perspective it gives us on problems. When a dog does something we don't like we calmly say to ourselves, "The dog is doing X. I would like him to do Y. How will I help him to make that change?" It's so understanding, so humane, so respectful—and so effective. We don't waste time and energy fuming over his naughtiness. We don't judge him to be bad because he's engaging in undesirable behavior. We assume he can do better, and we see our task as one of enacting and supporting change.

I urge you to view your human clients this way, too. Dog professionals tend to spend a lot of energy on their feelings about their clients. It's easy to be judgmental of people's attitudes toward their dogs, or their treatment of them. It's easy to be frustrated by their lack of skill or progress. But spending too much time on these emotions generally means missing solutions. When we decide a dog is a bad dog, we limit our options for treatment. Such a judgment of temperament often leads to a battle of wills. This is so much less useful than "The dog is doing X. I would like him to do Y. How will I help him to make that change?" It's similar with humans. When we decide a client is bad or stubborn or stupid, it leaves us with few options.

How different if, instead, we see their potential. "My client is now doing X when her dog does not sit. I would like her to do Y. How will I help her to make this change?" Or, "my client now believes X about dog behavior. I want her to understand Y. How will I help her to make this change?" Now you're cooking—you have a clearly stated question for which to generate an answer. You can formulate a game plan instead of throwing up your hands in despair. As an industry we've learned to show dogs compassion and patience while we work to change their behavior. Our behavior modification plans demonstrate a step by step approach and the understanding that solid changes in behavior can take time. Try approaching the human component of training the same way—it will temper your expectations, keeping frustration at bay.

People can learn new ideas and acquire new skills. Be patient, and remember to notice your clients' little changes, their bits of progress, and reinforce those—just as you would with a dog.

CASE STUDY

Stuart despaired after his first solo public class session with dogs. He lamented, "I just don't understand it! I told them at orientation—I explained all about punishment, and all about Gentle Leaders and everything, but two people—they still brought their dogs in on choke chains!" After he calmed down we talked for a while about his goals for his students and about the various reasons why they might be using choke chains. Then we laid out a game plan for gently moving the clients towards equipment alternatives and a new way of thinking about training. Stuart reported back to me at the end of the class. Beaming, he said, "One is using a GL and the other is using an Easy Walk harness! And last night at graduation I heard one of the parents telling all the other students about how great the GL is and recommending it to them! I think they're both going to sign up for the next class!"

Performance expectations—homework, progress, etc.

In the world of dog training one size rarely fits all. The ideal behavior modification or training plan from a professional perspective may not work in a home environment, particularly if we are talking about a typical American household with busy schedules and a day-to-day life of barely contained chaos. We often discuss how to set dogs up for success—well, why not do the same for our human clients?

Wherever possible, design training plans with your clients' strengths and lifestyles in mind. The idea of "Nothing for Free" or "Some Things for Free" is a great example of this—the idea of asking a dog to practice behaviors in exchange for the small daily rewards of life—going through doors, being fed, being let off leash, having a ball thrown, etc. Many owners are likely to learn this way of interacting with their dogs more easily than changing their patterns to incorporate formal training sessions. Plus the dog learns obedience in daily situations, rather than with the attendant environmental cues of a training session. Designing plans that fit individual lifestyles takes extra creativity, but will greatly increase compliance.

Also attempt to give clients choices wherever possible. These might come in the form of service choices (such as in-home training versus day training versus board and train—see Chapter 7). Other choices might include the order of goals to address, how to structure training sessions, or a choice between exercises. Of course, some situations lend themselves to the giving of choices while others require a more set regimen.

Firing clients

If you want to enjoy your business for many years to come, I recommend not forcing yourself to work with dogs or humans that cause you undue stress. There is no failure involved in firing a dog or human client. It's unreasonable to think that every match will be perfect. If you have a dog who is not working out, whether because you don't feel safe, or feel that your skills aren't the right match, or even because you simply do not enjoy the dog's company, you do no kindness to yourself, the client, or the dog by continuing. And if a human client causes unwarranted worry or difficulty, whether due to lack of compliance or poor attitude or a personality clash, your business is better off in the long run if you sever the relationship.

Sometimes it makes sense to be straightforward with a client about why you are ending services. If you feel you are not the right match or that the dog is unhappy or unsafe, just say so. For example, perhaps an asocial dog is miserable in a pack walking or daycare setting. You've tried to incorporate her and make her comfortable, but you are not seeing progress. You might suggest private walks instead. If you feel a training case is not making progress, suggest another trainer who might have more experience with that type of issue.

When you are letting a client go for reasons that have more to do with the dog or owner, you have to decide how honest to be. If the dog is dangerous, it's your professional responsibility to say so, and to document this in writing for your own liability protection. When a human client has been difficult, being upfront is a bit harder. If it's an issue of compliance, I would advise being honest, but if you're dealing with a temperament or personality issue, you may not feel comfortable saying so—and often that approach is not constructive anyway. To avoid unnecessary conflict you can use a general deflection—that you don't feel the progress being made is satisfactory, or that the group you're walking is not a good match for the dog, or that your schedule has changed such that you cannot accommodate daily visits to their home, etc.

Be the expert, be the professional, take charge

Remember that you are the expert, and let that govern your behavior with clients. I don't mean to suggest being pushy, bossy, condescending, or arrogant. I mean for you to be professional. For example, when you are doing a phone interview avoid behaving as though you're on a job interview. You are the professional. Take control of the interview—be the interviewer instead of the interviewee. You aren't begging for a job; you're screening a potential client. And when you go to a client's home, set the tone from the beginning. For example, after the initial hellos, gently but firmly take charge: "Shall we sit at the kitchen table?" Then set the expectations. Trainers might say something like, "As I described on the phone, I'd like to take some time to get more detailed information on what's going on with Pongo. Then we can discuss options for meeting your goals." Walkers, you might begin with, "The purpose of my interview is to learn more about Otis so that I can be sure to place him with other dogs whose company he will enjoy."

By setting the tone from the beginning you will be more easily able to direct the conversation and gather the information you need. Your confidence also helps clients build their confidence in you, which is particularly helpful when you suggest further services or are introducing them to a philosophy of training or care that is new to them.

CASE STUDY

Janet was furious. She had had her third session with Rich and his dog Hooch, and Rich's treatment of her had been rude, disrespectful, and dismissive. "I start to tell him about the next exercise when he interrupts me and says, 'Naw, I don't want to do that. Let's do something else.' And he keeps calling me 'Girl' and telling me that this 'treat slinging' isn't real training. He doesn't do any homework, but keeps letting me come back. It's infuriating." After some reflection on the situation and its causes, we made a game plan. Janet strode into the next appointment with confident posture and said firmly, before Rich had a chance to speak, "You are paying me for professional training services, for which I am certified and highly qualified. You have said you would like your dog to listen to you and be more focused. I can help you make that happen, but you will have to follow my instructions. If you find you cannot or will

> not, then you will need to find another trainer, as I
> have many clients who would like the benefit of my
> services." Without a hint of a pause, she continued,
> "Now, today we will work on three exercises. The
> first one looks like this..." She later laughed about
> the change in Rich. "He still tests me a bit from time
> to time, but overall he follows my lead, and he and
> Hooch are making a lot of progress. The best part is
> when I hear him tell his wife the things I've told him.
> Of course, he makes it sound like the ideas are all
> his, but that's okay with me!"

Don't let clients dictate your services

It can be tempting to say yes to things you didn't originally mean to do, especially at the outset when business is slow and anxiety high. But if your business is built for group walks, say no to the individual walk. If you mean for your pet sitting visits to run 30 minutes twice a day, don't let a potential client badger you into four 15-minute stops. This goes for policies, too. If you set your policies with purpose, stick to them. Your pick-up and drop-off times exist for a reason, as does your requirement of a minimum number of walks or daycare visits per week. Calmly and confidently explain to clients asking for a different service or policy exception that you are not able to accommodate that request, why you do things the way you do, and how doing so benefits them and/or their dogs. Making exceptions to your intended services and your policies may seem prudent when you're just starting out, but doing so will leave you with a clientele accustomed to ignoring your rules and a deeply flawed schedule. As you grow busier these problems will come to a head, and fixing them is much harder than avoiding them in the first place.

Work with clients who are right for you

It's also tempting, especially in the beginning, to take on all clients who come your way. But to do so will make your job harder and will eventually force you to make and implement difficult, sometimes even heart-wrenching decisions. So have a clear vision in mind of what clients—human and canine—are right for your business. What are you looking for in a daycare candidate? What kinds of training cases are you comfortable tackling? How do you want to be treated by your clients? What sorts of dog behavior can you tolerate in your home boarding environment? Craft your intake procedures to help you screen accordingly, and trust your gut, too. When that little voice tells you a person or dog may not be a good fit, listen. You don't have to be everything to everyone, and trying to be will only cause burnout.

Be the trainer

As I mentioned in Chapter 7, it's long been the default for trainers to teach clients how to train their dogs. But day training and board and train are rapidly gaining popularity as preferred training service models, and for good reason. Most dog owners don't want to become junior dog trainers. They want a professional to solve their dog training problem, just as we want an accountant to do our taxes rather than teach us how, a plumber to fix our pipes rather than coach us to do so on our own, or a lawyer to argue our case rather than give us written instructions on how we might proceed ourselves. I'm hard-pressed to think of another professional service industry where the model is to teach and require clients to perform the skilled work of its professionals themselves.

If you want to give clients the best chance of seeing behavioral change in their dogs, and yourself the best chance of making a good living as a dog trainer, I urge you to step up and be the dog trainer by doing as much of the training yourself as possible. It will be a huge relief to your busy, harried clients and you're likely to find selling your services easier. After all, who wants to be told they'll spend money in order to be given weekly homework to perform someone else's job? You will have to design your service appropriately to provide enough transfer support—after all, if the dog doesn't learn to behave differently for the client, and the client doesn't learn how to maintain the changes you've trained, all will be for naught. But you should find teaching your clients how to maintain the training you've done significantly easier than teaching them to install the training themselves. You'll enjoy much higher client compliance, too.

Charge what you're worth

Go back and re-read the rates section in Chapter 7. Remind yourself that you are worth what you charge and that you needn't apologize for being paid for your professional knowledge and skill. The impact you have on the lives of your clients and their dogs is worth every penny they spend for your expertise, and it will be difficult to attract serious clients if you price yourself too low. I know you want to help as many dogs as possible, but you're also running a business. The good news is that you can do both. In fact, the more business you have, the more people and dogs you will help. And the longer you stay in business, the more dogs you'll help over time. If you burn out over financial stress or are forced to take a job or return to a previous career, you lose your ability to have the same amount of impact. So no more guilt—charge what you're worth and know you're worth it.

Sell confidently

Start with a perspective shift. Whether you're responding to an initial inquiry on the phone or via email, or meeting a potential client for an intake interview, view the conversation as a screening process, not a job interview. Remember that they contacted you. They have a problem—a behavior issue or upcoming trip or long hours at work—and you have a solution via your training program, sitting or boarding service, or daycare or walking business. Let people know how you can help, actively offer your service, and don't be afraid to make specific recommendations for what you think will best fit their needs. People respond to confidence and assurance. Fake it at first if you have to. Your confidence will grow as your sales do.

Trainers, whatever service model you offer—coaching, day training, or board and train—sell your clients the amount of training needed to give them the best chance of success in reaching their training goals. Letting clients choose less training than you know is required sets everyone—them, their dog, and you—up for failure. No doctor would ask a patient how many chemo sessions they'd like. No lawyer lets a client dictate the number of hours it will take to prepare their case. You're the expert, you're the professional. It's up to you to set clients up for success by telling them—and selling them—what is required to meet their goals.

"Oh! You're a dog trainer! My dog does this thing…" Avoid giving away free advice

We've all been there—at a party, or in line at the grocery store, or at a child's soccer game. Wherever it happens, you know how it goes. Someone asks you what you do. You tell them. Next thing you know you're listening to their dog problems and being pumped for free advice. And it's a funny thing—we often feel compelled to give it. Sometimes because we don't know how to get out of doing so, sometimes because we love what we do and enjoy talking about it, and often because we care about dogs and want to see them get the help they need.

But it's a losing proposition for all involved to give free advice. It cheats you out of business and devalues your professional knowledge and skill, it reduces the chance the dog owner will pursue the help he or she needs, and it doesn't get the dog any real help. Advice given in a social situation is seldom followed—and you can't offer the kind of detail and support that most cases require.

Setting boundaries for public and social spaces

Few people are aware of the level of education and experience a qualified trainer possesses, of the amount of information needed to diagnose a behavior, and of the degree of thought put into a behavior modification plan. As a result, they don't feel shy about asking for quick-fix tips. The trick to handling these situations is to politely avoid giving too much free advice while creating the highest likelihood that they will actually seek your professional help. Here is a strategy you can try:

1. Interrupt

2. Empathize

3. Build confidence

4. Redirect

5. Tip (optional)

6. End

Interrupt. Let's say a woman begins her story, "My little dog Rin Tin Tin barks so loudly you'd think she was a German Shepherd, or even two dogs! Drives me crazy. She barks all day long. One time she even..."

This is a good time for Step 1, the interruption. Allow the other person to tell just enough of the story to give you a hint of the problem, but don't let her get going full swing. The more she invests in the story, the harder it will be for you to avoid the request for immediate answers and explanations. Intervene in a friendly and assertive manner, and try to be reinforcing to soften the interruption. "Sounds like Rin Tin Tin is quite the character! Amazing how little dogs can have such big personalities."

Empathize. Immediately make it clear that you've heard their concern: "Barking, especially when it's constant, can be so frustrating! It's hard to hear yourself think!"

Build confidence. This is the time to elegantly let them know you're an expert and that diagnosis and treatment is taken seriously in the world of professional dog training. "That kind of barking can be many things—demand barking, barrier frustration, alarm barking, separation anxiety…"

Redirect. This is your opportunity to suggest your services, which also gently but clearly implies that you require payment for your expertise. "To know for sure what makes Rin Tin Tin bark, I would need to do a complete diagnostic interview. Then I can work with you to design a treatment plan to best suit your needs. Here's my card if you'd like to do that. You can also take a look at my website to learn a little more about what I do and to see my background and credentials. I'd be delighted to work with you and Rin Tin Tin to see if we can't create a nice, quiet house for you."

If you're really gung-ho and have a feeling they wouldn't mind, you might ask for their contact information (but don't scribble on the backs of receipts, carry around a small book for this) so you can follow up with them.

Tip (optional). If you think it's warranted, tip them by offering a management or training suggestion. An example for Rin Tin Tin's mom might be, "In the meantime, here's one thing you can do that might help: Reward him any time he's not barking. If you notice the house is quiet, take a moment to give him a cookie or a belly rub. Let him know that you appreciate the peace." Depending on the situation, your aim could be to offer a measure with immediate effect in order to build confidence in your ability to help. Other times you might present a management suggestion to diminish risk or to create some improvement in the life of either the owner or the dog.

End. It's important now to end the conversation. If you don't, it's likely the person will jump in to ask follow-up questions or tell you additional information or stories about their dog, which puts you right back in the hot seat. If you're in a situation where you can walk away, do so. "It was really nice meeting you and hearing about Rin Tin Tin. I hope you'll let me know if I can be of help. Have a great day now!" If you're trapped—in a line or waiting room, for example, change the subject. "By the way, do you happen to know what the weather is supposed to be like this weekend? I've been hearing all sorts of conflicting reports. I'm putting on a birthday party this weekend and not sure whether to plan it for inside or out in the garden. It's for my little niece. If she had it her way, we'd..."

Additional advice on giving advice

Though the six steps are broken down for you here, in practice they run together and overlap. Try not to pause, as a determined dog storyteller always will look for a way back in. And practice makes perfect—though it may seem a little silly, try practicing this technique in the shower or while you're driving. Recall a past situation where you were ambushed with "A dog trainer! My dog..." story. Re-enact the scene in your head with these six steps. The more you train yourself to respond this way, the easier it'll be next time you find yourself cornered at a dinner party.

Finally, be aware of the ethical and liability issues that sometimes lurk in these conversations. For example, if the situation described to you is potentially dangerous for the dog or other people, or if it sounds like the dog's quality of life is threatened, you may feel compelled to have a longer discussion. But be careful—advice given in public or social contexts can never be as complete as you would want it to be, and you do not have a contract to help cover your liability. Center your advice in Step 5 (Tipping) around management suggestions to reduce any potential risk to the dog or humans. You may want to use Steps 2, 3, and 4 (Empathizing, Building Confidence, and Redirecting) to attempt to impress the seriousness of the situation upon them. Be firm but gentle, as some people may not be ready to hear the bad news. If they feel overwhelmed or perceive an attack they will be less likely to call you or another trainer for help. Ask for contact information so you can follow up and schedule a proper consultation.

Walkers, sitters, and daycare operators—be particularly careful in giving training advice in social or professional situations. Without certification you may be at a higher level of liability risk if you give advice that spills over into areas of training. It's safer and more appropriate to refer clients to a dog trainer for training questions.

Setting boundaries for friends and family

The above strategy becomes a lot harder to use when friends and family are involved. But it's very important to have boundaries here, too—especially if you have a lot of friends and family members who have dogs! Dealing with the problem dogs of loved ones can be a serious source of burnout for several reasons; for one thing, friends and family often have the worst compliance, perhaps because there's no sense of urgency—you'll always be there. Also, research shows that people in our culture simply don't value what they don't pay for, including advice. And that double whammy—lack of compliance and lack of professional regard—can cause tension. It's frustrating to see your advice ignored, and I've seen cases where family or friends blame the trainer when the problem isn't solved, even when the cause of failure is a clear lack of compliance. You can imagine the painful dynamics there. In summary, if you have heard the sayings about not working with family or living with friends, add to that not training friends' and family members' dogs.

But how do you avoid it? Gingerly would be an understatement. Try to think (and I urge you to do this proactively if it's not too late) of an explanation that would make sense to that person, and come across as supportive and caring, and not as a brush off. Some I have suggested to others in that situation have included:

- "I feel I'm too close to you and Tramp to get a good perspective on this (or to be effective)…Let me find another trainer to bring in for a fresh set of eyes."

- "This is a little out of my area of knowledge or expertise. I know this awesome trainer who would be able to help. Let me go grab her number."

- "I won't be able to give you the help you need over the phone—this is something that really needs doing in person. Let me find a good trainer in your area."

If these don't feel like they'd work for you, think about the specifics of your case and look for the out. And of course if you can just talk straight—"I have this policy, and here's why…" that's great.

Certainly there will be cases you feel comfortable taking or are compelled to accept. I hope you'll keep them to an absolute minimum, but if you do find yourself in that situation, follow your best practices. Set a professional tone at the beginning of each session and do not allow yourself to be pulled off topic. And try not to talk about the training much in between sessions. If you see your dad or sister at the dinner table and they start asking follow up questions, cut it off with some version of "Hmm… interesting. Let me think about that when I have my trainer brain on and I'll come up with something for our next session."

CASE STUDY

I was talking about burnout to a group of dog trainers preparing to graduate from an advanced training program, and Amanda nodded her head gravely when I spoke about the dangers of working with friends and family. "You have a story, I take it?" She laughed. "Boy, do I! When I was a newlywed I agreed to do some training for my husband's parents. Their little dog was still urinating in the house on a frequent basis—and was four years old. So I went over the whole housetraining protocol for them, even lent them a crate and got the dog used to it. They quickly undid her comfort with the crate by using it as a punishment—even though I warned against that—and, three years later, she's still peeing in the house. Which means that at every family function I get a full report on my failure as a trainer: 'Well, Petunia peed in Harvey's den again this morning, and she still won't go near that box you brought over!' Drives me crazy! At first, I would try to re-explain, to remind them of the steps, but my mother in law would just say, 'No, we already tried that—you said that last time.' I can tell you, avoid working for friends or family if you possibly can!"

Pro bono work

I generally discourage pro bono work. Many of my clients want to help people who cannot afford professional services, and I commend that. But as a way of serving this goal, pro bono work—offering your services to individuals for free—has many unintended consequences.

One concern is compliance burnout. We often do not value what we don't pay for, and many trainers find that pro bono clients have a low rate of compliance. Now there are exceptions to this, too. A lot depends on how you screen your clients. Pro bono clients who are truly in financial need but very committed to their animals can be the best clients you'll ever have. I have also seen many trainers talked down in their prices or into fully pro bono work by people who perhaps did not truly meet the standards of financial hardship but instead were clever bargain hunters, and the results were frustrating.

But it is always a dilemma. How can you really screen individuals without asking for financial records? It's tough, and there are many legal implications in setting up such a system.

The other potential hazard with pro bono work is getting a reputation for it. If you are trying to run a business for income you do not want to become known as the go-to person for pro bono work. Your phone will soon be ringing off the hook as every trainer in your area sends people your way who have balked at their prices or shared a sob story.

If you want to dedicate a portion of your time to less privileged dog owners consider volunteering your time rather than offering pro bono services. Volunteer to answer a hotline at the local shelter, or to make yourself available there for public training on certain days for a set number of hours. This way the shelter can do the screening and you can offer your services without tripping up your own business.

If you do choose to engage in pro bono work, set clear boundaries. For example, give yourself a rule of no more than X number of pro bono cases at any given time.

Don't try to do everything yourself

When you run a small business you have to oversee everything. You may be an excellent dog walker but are you ready to be a bookkeeper, accountant, marketing manager, secretary, and office manager? A key to successful full-time business ownership is to recognize your weaknesses and hire help for tasks that confound you or that require expertise you don't possess.

List the skills required to run your business. Then ask yourself: what are you good at? Where do your interests lie? Which tasks can you readily do? Which will stress you, weaken the business, or possibly be left undone? For those, get help. Trade skills with a friend or hire a contractor or professional service provider.

Take a vacation

I can't tell you how many dog pros have told me over the years that they haven't had a vacation in years. Clients and seminar attendees often try to tell me that it's "impossible" to take a vacation in this industry. Not true. It's actually quite easy: Turn the pages of your calendar until you reach a stretch that is not yet burdened by obligations. Black out as many days as you dare. Put out a letter to clients letting them know you'll be taking a vacation and, if you don't have staff who can cover your absence, that you want to give them plenty of notice to make alternate arrangements during that time. (You will likely be pleasantly surprised by how many send their support, even telling you that it's "about time" or "well-deserved.") Then take the vacation. That's it. Come back refreshed, with renewed energy to push your business forward. You may worry about the impact of taking a break, but the truth is you and your business will be healthier for it.

11

Parting Shots: A Few Extra Pieces of Advice

For most people starting a business is fraught with anxiety. You work so hard and can't help but have expectations and hopes for things to come along quickly—particularly clients and revenue!—and despair sets in fast when they don't. I've seen people give up on their businesses far too soon because the pressure got to them—but there is no reason to let that happen to you.

The six month rule

First, set reasonable expectations. Anticipate that any marketing effort you make will take a minimum of six months to begin yielding results, if not a year. If that seems like a long time to you, it might help to envision how marketing works. Say a potential client picks up your brochure with the intention of calling, but happens to place it beneath the take-out menus, only to uncover it months later and think, "You know, I should really do that!" Or someone takes home a class schedule but finds she's just too busy to fit anything new in—until her dog steals the Thanksgiving turkey and she decides she's had enough and where did she put that flyer? Another person might have read your first two newsletters at his vet's office, but it was the article on resource guarding in the third one that prompted him to call. Just because the phone doesn't ring as soon as you make your efforts doesn't mean it won't. Give people time to think about things and to need your services.

Ride the waves

But you don't have to just sit and wait, either—nor should you. Remember from Chapter 4 the importance of marketing. Implement a marketing project and then, while you're waiting to see how it goes, start the next project on your list. Once that's underway, begin marketing project number three.

Marketing in waves has two advantages for you. First, it keeps you busy while you wait. There is no better antidote to the stresses of waiting than productive activity. Second, it helps your business grow faster and more consistently as each marketing wave, or project, hits the shore, bringing additional clients. Consistent marketing helps smooth out some of the client dry spells that often plague dog pros. You're also hedging your bets—if one project's results are disappointing, another is right on its heels to help.

Trainer error or, "it's not working!"

When something isn't working, positive reinforcement trainers know to look at themselves before blaming the dog or owner. Was there trainer error? Before you decide your business success is impossible, check for a dog pro error before giving up. Are you truly putting in the marketing effort and time? Are your efforts in line with the marketing maxims laid out in Chapter 4? Have you set at least three waves in motion and waited six months to a year for the effect?

Eventually you can go into a maintenance mode with your marketing, simply renewing the initiatives that have proved the most fruitful. But in the beginning, or anytime you look for active growth, keep busy and be patient.

Click yourself—keeping perspective

I've found that many of my clients over the years are quick to disparage themselves and focus on the negative in the first couple years of owning a business. When you're having a rough day, or week, try giving yourself a little R+—remember, positive reinforcement is powerful stuff! Literally sit down with paper and pen and list the things you've gotten done, milestones you've hit, efforts you've made, things you've learned, clients you've helped. Note how far you have come. Sometimes when things don't happen at the speed we wish for it feels like nothing is happening at all. But you may be surprised by the progress you are making if you stop to click yourself for it.

Resources

1. Business Resources

Insurance Agents
Dennis Stowers dstowers@mourer-foster.com
800-686-2663 ext. 230

Legal Assistance
General:
Heidi Meinzer
heidi@meinzerlaw.com
www.meinzerlaw.com

Trademarks:
Legal Care for Your Business and Product Name www.nolo.com

Employee and Independent Contractor Issues:
The Employer's Legal Handbook, www.nolo.com
Hiring Independent Contractors, www.nolo.com

Contracts:
Business Toolkit for Trainers, www.dogtec.org
Business Toolkit for Walkers & Sitters, www.dogtec.org
Business Toolkit for Daycare & Boarding, www.dogtec.org

Bookkeepers and Accountants
Dollars & Scents, www.dog-pro-cpa.com
A full service bookkeeping and tax preparation service exclusively for dog professionals

Bookkeeping Help, www.bookkeepinghelp.com
US and Canadian directory for bookkeepers, accountants, and tax preparers

Market Research
www.demographicsnow.com

Your local Chamber of Commerce

Marketing Writers and Designers
dog*tec maintains an active, up-to-date list of writers, logo designers, and website developers who specialize in working with dog businesses. Email info@dogtec.org or call 510-525-2547 for free referrals.

Online Marketing Opportunities
Dogasaur, www.dogasaur.com

Dog Groomers, www.doggroomers.com

Dog Seminars Directory, www.dogseminarsdirectory.com

Dog Trainers Directory, www.dogtrainersdirectory.com

Dogwalker.com, www.dogwalker.com

Embarkly, www.embarkly.com

Find Pet Care, www.findpetcare.com

Red Dog Classifieds, www.reddogclassifieds.com

Rover.com, www.rover.com

Software and Apps
123 Pet Software, www.123petsoftware.com (groomers, boarders)

Appointment Plus, www.appointment-plus.com (groomers)

Betta Walka, www.bettawalka.com (walkers)

Blue Wave Professional Pet Sitter, www.professionalpetsitter.com (sitters)

Dog Biz Pro, www.dogbizpro.com (trainers)

Dog Trainer Connexion, www.dogtrainerconnexion.com (trainers)

Groomer's Advantage, www.groomersassistant.com (groomers)

Groom Pro, www.groom-pro.com (groomers)

ICE for Pets app, www.iceforpets.com (walkers, sitters)

K9 Bytes, www.k9bytessoftware.com (daycare, boarders)

Kennel Master, www.kennelmaster-software.com (boarders)

Paw Loyalty software, www.pawloyalty.com (walkers, sitters)

PetExec, www.petexec.net (daycares, boarders, groomers, trainers, retail)

PetPro Software, www.petprosoftware.net (walkers, sitters)

Petschedule, www.petschedule.com (groomers, boarders)

Pet Sit Click software, www.petsitclick.com (walkers, sitters)

PetTech PetSaver app, www.pettech.net (walkers, sitters, daycares, boarders)

Power Pet Sitter ,www.powerpetsitter.com (sitters)

Snaggle Foot Dog Walks & Pet Care, www.snagglefoot.com (walkers, sitters)

Thoughtful Systems, www.thoughtfulsystems.com (walkers)

Ubooq, www.ubooq.com (groomers)

Veriwalk app, www.veriwalk.com

dog*tec Business Support Services
www.dogtec.org

info@dogtec.org, veronica@dogtec.org

- Business and marketing consulting
- Support products, including the Business Toolkit, Homework Toolkit, BMod Toolkit, Open Enrollment Puppy Curriculum Package, Open Enrollment Basic Manners

Curriculum Package, Topics Classes Curriculum Package, and Marketing Toolkit

• Free *Monthly Minute* email business newsletter—sign up for a free subscription at www.dogtec.org

2. Education Resources for Trainers

Training Schools
Academy for Dog Trainers with Jean Donaldson (online course)
www.academyfordogtrainers.com

Animal Behavior College (online course augmented with local mentorships)   www.animalbehaviorcollege.com

Canine Behavior & Training Academy with Denise Mazzola, Keene, NH   www.denisemazzola.com

CATCH Canine Trainers Academy (online course augmented with optional local mentorships)   www.catchdogtrainers.com

Canine Behavior Academy with Trish King, San Francisco Bay Area
www.canine-behavior-associates.com

Coaching People to Train Their Dogs Course with Terry Ryan, Sequim, WA   www.legacycanine.com

Dog Training Internship Academy, San Francisco Bay Area and additional locations   www.dogtraininginternshipacademy.com

Gail Fisher's All Dogs Academy, Manchester, NH
www.alldogsacademy.com

Instructor's Training Course with Pia Silvani, various locations
www.dogsofcourse.com

Karen Pryor Academy, various locations   www.clickertraining.com

Peaceable Paws with Pat Miller, Hagerstown, MD and Murphy, NC
www.peaceablepaws.com

Raising Canine Beginning Dog Trainer's Course (online course)
www.raisingcanine.com

Continuing Education Seminars
Association of Pet Dog Trainers (web seminars and annual conference)   www.apdt.com

Dog Seminars Directory (a list of seminars taking place throughout the country) www.dogseminarsdirectory.com

Dogs of Course www.dogsofcourse.com

dog*tec (classes and web seminars) www.dogtec.org

International Association of Animal Behavior Consultants (web seminars and annual conference) www.iaabc.org

Positively Trained www.positivelytrained.com

Puppyworks www.puppyworks.com

Raising Canine (telecourses) www.raisingcanine.com

Recommended Books
This is by no means a comprehensive list and you shouldn't stop here!

Aggressive Behavior in Dogs: A Comprehensive Technical Manual for Professionals, James O'Heare

Canine Body Language: A Photographic Guide, Brenda Aloff

Culture Clash, Jean Donaldson

Coaching People to Train Their Dogs, Terry Ryan

Dog Language: An Encyclopedia of Canine Behavior, 2nd Edition, Roger Abrantes

Dogs Behaving Badly, Nicholas Dodman

The Domestic Dog, James Serpell

Don't Shoot the Dog, Karen Pryor

Exel-erated Learning, Pam Reid

How to Teach an Old Dog New Tricks, Ian Dunbar

Minding Your Dog Business, Veronica Boutelle and Rikke Jorgensen

The Power of Positive Training, Pat Miller

Book and DVD Sources

Dogwise www.dogwise.com

Tawzer Video www.tawzerdogvideos.com

Associations, Accreditation

Certification Council for Professional Dog Trainers: www.ccpdt.org

Association of Pet Dog Trainers www.apdt.com

International Association of Animal Behavior Consultants: www.iaabc.org

For Dog Walkers and Daycares

I've placed dog walkers and daycares together because their educational needs are so similar—a real emphasis on dog-dog behavior, pack composition and management, and reading body language.

Schools and Accreditation

dog*tec Dog Walking Academy www.dogtec.org (multiple locations)

The Dog Gurus Courses (for daycares) www.safeoffleashdogplay.com (online)

Continuing Education Seminars, Books, & DVDs

The Business Of Dog Walking: How to Make a Living Doing What You Love, Veronica Boutelle

Canine Body Language: A Photographic Guide, Brenda Aloff

Dog Language: An Encyclopedia of Canine Behavior, 2nd Edition, Roger Abrantes

Off Leash Dog Play—A Complete Guide to Safety and Fun, Robin K. Bennett & Susan Briggs

For Pet Sitters
Education Seminars
Association of Pet Sitting Excellence (annual online conference, web seminars) www.petsittingexcellence.com

National Association of Professional Pet Sitters (annual conference)

www.petsitters.org

Pet Sitters International (annual conference) www.petsit.com

Pet Sitting Live (annual conference) www.petsittinglive.com

Basic dog training education will be helpful, too—see resources above.

Books
Pet Sitting for Profit, Patti Moran

Associations and Accreditation
Association of Pet Sitting Excellence www.petsittingexcellence.com

National Association of Professional Pet Sitters (NAPPS) www.petsitters.org

Pet Sitters International (PSI) www.petsit.com

3. Budget Considerations
A word on business plans and budgets: Unless you are seeking fund-ing, you will not need a formal business plan. Following the advice in each chapter of this book will reward you with an informal busi-ness plan to guide you as you move forward to start or grow your enterprise. Should you require a formal plan, you'll soon realize that there are more templates to choose from than you could possibly need. It's best to ask the funding sources you will be petitioning what they want to see in a solid plan. If they have a specific template, all the better. In the absence of such direction, Palo Alto Software has a good product with several dog-related samples: www.paloalto.com.

Here I have provided a basic list of potential start-up and ongoing costs you should be aware of when doing your feasibility math.

Start-Up Costs
Vehicle (if needed)

Facility (if using)
- initial lease money down or down payment for purchase
- build-out costs

Communication
  - phone installation and/or cell phone purchase
  - initial Internet fees—service installation

Initial Marketing
  - website development
  - URL purchase
  - design and printing
  - advertising, if applicable
  - other one time initial project costs specific to your plans

Professional Fees and Assistance
  - paperwork fees
  - contracts
  - accountancy support
  - lawyer, if using one

Education
  - school and seminar fees
  - books and DVDs
  - business coaching support

Office Supplies
  - hardware—computer, printer, etc.
  - software—Quickbooks Pro, kennel software if needed, etc.

Dog Supplies
  - trainers—training tools
  - walkers—leashes, tags, first aid kit, etc.
  - sitters—toys if using
  - daycares—beds, dishes, toys, training aids, first aid kit, etc.

Ongoing Costs
Vehicle
  - maintenance
  - gas

Facility, if using
- lease or mortgage
- utilities
- phone
- repair and maintenance
- insurance

Communication
- cell phone
- Internet service

Marketing
- website maintenance, hosting fees, URL renewal
- ongoing project costs
- replacement printing
- advertising, if applicable

Professional Fees and Assistance
- professional insurance
- accountancy and/or bookkeeping

Professional Development and Continuing Education
- association fees
- seminars (don't forget travel expenses for conferences)
- books and DVDs
- business support services

Office Supplies

Dog Supplies
- trainers—treats, tools, etc.
- walkers—treats, replacement leashes, etc.
- sitters—treats and toys if using
- daycares—treats, food (if supplying), replacement beds, toys, etc.

Employment or Independent Contractor Costs, if using
- pay
- payroll taxes and fees

4. Annotated Start-Up To Do Lists
Legalities and Liabilities
See Chapter 3 for more detailed instructions.

	To Do	Notes	Source	X
1.	Check name availability	Be sure the name you want to use is free for use. Do a search on the national trade-mark sight, the state trademark and LLC/ corporation site, the county site, and check to see what domain names are available (.com, etc).	www.register.com or equivalent your secretary of state site your county clerk site www.godaddy.com or equivalent	
2.	File for LLC Status (op-tional)	This is an optional step you may choose to take to increase your liability protection. You can convert to an LLC at any time. If you file as an LLC be sure to use the full business name as the "applicant" on all other steps below.	Download forms from your secretary of state site For help: www.dogtec.org www.nolopress.com Local Lawyers	
3.	Business License	Remember to proactively file a home based business exemption if needed.	Download forms from your city website, call, or walk in	

	To Do	Notes	Source	X
4.	Fictitious Business Name	Read instructions carefully—multiple copies are often required. You will probably need to run an announcement in a local paper. If neither the FBN nor the business license need the other one completed first, go ahead and file both at the same time.	Download forms from your city website, call, or walk in	
5.	Get Your EIN	If you've filed as an LLC or if you plan to have employees you need an EIN. Otherwise it is not required. If you apply online the form number is SS-4	Apply online at:www.irs.gov Or get your EIN over the phone by calling 1 800 829 4933	
6.	Open Business Bank Account	This is highly recommended for all businesses and required for LLCs Call your bank ahead to schedule an appointment. Be sure to ask them what paperwork to bring along.	Local bank of choice	

	To Do	Notes	Source	X
7.	Join a Professional Association	This is great for continuing education opportunities and it helps to professionalize your business as well as push the industry forward. Membership also provides access to professional insurance.	www.apdt.com www.iaabc.com www.petsittingexcellence.com www.napps.com www.psi.com	
8.	Obtain Insurance	If you're going to see clients prior to this step, get insurance first. You can always change the name on your policy if you need to.	Agents: Dennis Stowers dstowers@mourer-foster.com	
9.	Purchase Contracts	Have contracts in hand before you see clients. If you will be seeing clients before this step, move this step up!	www.dogtec.org	
10.	Service Mark your Business Name (optional)	You can service mark at the state or national level. Both are optional. If you choose to pursue a national service mark you may want to engage legal assistance.	State: download forms from your secretary of state site National: www.uspto.gov Heidi Meinzer heidi@meinzerlaw.com www.meinzerlaw.com Kelly McCarthy kmccarthy@sideman.com www.sideman.com	

	To Do	Notes	Source	X
11.	Learn LLC Rules & Requirements	Learn what you need to know to keep your LLC protection intact.	www.dogtec.org www.NoloPress.com	

Marketing

While waiting for various paperwork to come back from the offices you've sent it out to, you can get to work on your marketing. See Chapter 4 for more detailed instructions.

	To Do	Notes	Source	X
1.	Define Your Services	Decide exactly what you're going to offer, down to the details. Consider a specialized niche. Be clear about who your target clients are.	www.dogtec.org	
2.	Develop Your Marketing Message	How will you describe what you do to those you want to use your services? What makes you different? What benefits do clients stand to gain?	www.dogtec.org	
3.	Develop Your Marketing Projects	These are the vehicles that will get your message out to your audience. Choose several projects and pick one or two to implement first.	www.dogtec.org	
4.	Develop Marketing Materials	Now that you know what your projects are, you know what materials you need. Engage a designer for a professionally branded look.	Email info@ dogtec.org for free referrals	

Rates, Policies, and Systems
See Chapter 7 for detailed instructions.

	To Do	Notes	Source	X
1.	Compare Local Rates	Call other local service providers (or ask a friend to call for you) to find out what they charge. Be sure to get details about their services—how much time they offer, number of sessions or walks, any extra materials, etc.		
2.	Set Your Rates	Keep all variables in mind; local rates, how your services are different or unique, what you need and want to be paid. You do not have to "apologize" for being new through your rates!	www.dogtec.org	
3.	Write Your Policies	Put together policies for payment, cancellation, geographical boundaries, and any packages you are offering. Write your policies for the future! You may not be busy now, but you will be. Make sure your policies will fit the needs of a growing business.	www.dogtec.org	
4.	Design Systems and Develop or Purchase Materials for Them	You need systems and materials for phone screening, your initial intake or interview process, payment and general bookkeeping, ongoing record keeping, dog groupings and routes if applicable, client homework if applicable, etc.	www.dogtec.org Quickbooks Pro software	

Scheduling
See Chapter 10 for more detailed instructions.

	To Do	Notes	X
1.	List All Business Duties	This includes client and dog care time as well as marketing and admin work.	
2.	List Everything Else	Include any other responsibilities, including any part or full time work, family duties, and recreational activities you wish to prioritize.	
3.	Devise a Schedule	Work to accommodate your business and personal needs as efficiently as possible.	
4.	Try It Out	Give the schedule a go and make adjustments as needed.	

5. Service Comparison Chart

Service	Best Suited For:	Best suited for clients who:	Relative client cost	Best suited for dog pros who:	Relative start up costs	Relative on-going costs:	Relative revenue potential *	Impact on time	Other Notes
Private Training: Coaching	obedience manners puppy raising home-based issues such as digging, separation anxiety, baby prep, house training, etc.	have time and a desire to be hands on have higher end skills	expensive	have strong coaching and interpersonal skills enjoy working with people	very low	very low	low	work is mostly nights and weekends	can be slower training process if seen all the way through, training is likely to last can be difficult to see the process all the way through

Service	Best Suited For:	Best suited for clients who:	Relative client cost	Best suited for dog pros who:	Relative start up costs	Relative on-going costs:	Relative revenue potential *	Impact on time	Other Notes
Private Training; Day Training	obedience long-winded, technical problems such as fear and aggression	have less time and more money want their dogs to remain at home	more expensive	enjoy flexible scheduling	very low	very low	moderate	work is done during daytime, when other training work is slow	can often see faster training results faster progress often means higher client compliance

Service	Best Suited For:	Best suited for clients who:	Relative client cost	Best suited for dog pros who:	Relative start up costs	Relative on-going costs:	Relative revenue potential *	Impact on time	Other Notes
Private Training: Board & Train	obedience manners aggression	have less time and more money want immediate results	more expensive	enjoy more hands on time with dogs actively enjoy company of dogs prefer less time working with clients	very low in home high in facility	very low in home high in facility	high	at home: always "at work," home/work boundaries blurred at home: can work at off hours at facility: overnight care required	can be lucrative but also stressful due to lack of down time can be a quicker approach for training results

Service	Best Suited For:	Best suited for clients who:	Relative client cost	Best suited for dog pros who:	Relative start up costs	Relative on-going costs:	Relative revenue potential *	Impact on time	Other Notes
Group Classes	basic obedience manners puppies some dog-dog re-activity tricks, sports, specialty classes	have time and desire to actively work with their dogs	less expensive	have strong teaching and coaching skills have strong organizational skills	low to high depending on space costs	low to high depending on space costs	low to moderate depending on number of classes	work is mostly nights and weekends	great way to impact multiple dogs and people at once can be a good marketing opportunity for other services

Service	Best Suited For:	Best suited for clients who:	Relative client cost	Best suited for dog pros who:	Relative start up costs	Relative ongoing costs:	Relative revenue potential *	Impact on time	Other Notes
Off Leash Group Walks	social, active dogs dogs who require higher level of exercise	are unable to get dogs out due to work or infirmity have a steady income	ongoing	have strong dog skills, ability to read dog body language enjoy being outdoors and exercising are calm and able to handle the unexpected	very low unless purchasing a vehicle	low to medium depending on gas usage	moderate	work is all done during the day time used very efficiently	time spent outside generally makes up for time in car bad weather can be difficult

Service	Best Suited For:	Best suited for clients who:	Relative client cost	Best suited for dog pros who:	Relative start up costs	Relative ongoing costs:	Relative revenue potential*	Impact on time	Other Notes
On Leash Individual Walks	older dogs; asocial dogs; dogs with fear or aggression issues	work long hours; have a steady income	ongoing	prefer less challenge and risk than group walks; enjoy working with dogs one on one	very low	very low	low	can be relatively inefficient time to revenue ratio	lots of time spent in car; scheduling can be tricky
On Leash Group Walks	very well socialized dogs; very leash savvy dogs	work long hours; have a steady income	ongoing	have an excellent sense of humor; have strong leash handling skills; do not have access to off leash areas	very low	very low	low to moderate	can be an efficient use of time	multiple leashed dogs can be difficult to manage

Service	Best Suited For:	Best suited for clients who:	Relative client cost	Best suited for dog pros who:	Relative start up costs	Relative ongoing costs:	Relative revenue potential *	Impact on time	Other Notes
Boarding in Your Home	social dogs if you have your own dogs dogs with special needs	want to know their dog is receiving home style care	more expensive	enjoy the company of extra dogs in their home	very low	very low	moderate	work/home boundaries blurred can work on own schedule	can be lucrative but also stressful due to lack of down time
House Sitting	dogs with special needs asocial dogs	want their dog in its own environment want their house looked after	expensive	enjoy working in others' homes enjoy working with a variety of animals	very low	very low	low	potential for working during the day	time spent away from home can lead to burnout not conducive for home relationships and having ones own pets

Service	Best Suited For:	Best suited for clients who:	Relative client cost	Best suited for dog pros who:	Relative start up costs	Relative on-going costs:	Relative revenue potential *	Impact on time	Other Notes
Drop In Sitting	dogs who can tolerate long hours alone	need short term services are on a budget	less expensive	enjoy working with a variety of animals	very low	moderate due to gas usage	low to moderate	can be relatively inefficient time to revenue ration lots of night, early morning, and weekend work	lots of time spent in car
Daycare	very social dogs with no serious behavior issues	work long hours have a steady income	ongoing	have strong dog skills, ability to read dog body language enjoy the company of groups of dogs	high	high	moderate	must be at facility long days M-F	some find daycare fascinating, others become bored and miss human company

Service	Best Suited For:	Best suited for clients who:	Relative client cost	Best suited for dog pros who:	Relative start up costs	Relative on-going costs:	Relative revenue potential *	Impact on time	Other Notes
Facility Boarding	social dogs dogs with no serious behavior issues are preferable	do not want dog left in home while they are away want to keep cost relatively low	less expensive to expensive	enjoy daily ongoing company of dogs	high	high	moderate to high	conscientious boarding requires 24 hour attendance	round the clock working can lead to burnout

NOTE: Revenue potential is relative to other services on the chart, and to relative time to revenue ratio (time needed to generate the revenue), and based on a single person business. For example, one person walking two groups of dogs off leash can make a moderate income. Hiring additional people to walk for them could result in a high or even very high income.

169

6. ROI (Return on Investment) Tracking Sheet

Use something similar to this sheet to track how people heard about you, and the outcome of the contact. This will give you data to use when determining where to put additional marketing resources.

Date	Name	How Heard	They Their Needs	Outcome	Outcome Date	Notes
4/10/14	Barbara Polino	newsletter in Best Care Vet's office	Yorkie is resource guarding	hired for 8 session training package	4/18/14	
4/11/14	Ted Mackey	SPCA referral	8 mos old not coming when called	enrolled in adolescent manners class	4/11/14	Took adult basic class afterward

About the Author

Veronica Boutelle, MA Ed., CTC, is the founder of dog*tec, the dog pro industry's leading business consultancy, through which she has been helping dog professionals create their dream businesses since 2003. Veronica is a sought-after speaker at conferences and dog training schools across the country and internationally. She writes the business column for the Association of Pet Dog Trainer's *Chronicle of the Dog* and her articles regularly appear in many other dog industry publications. Veronica's other books include *Minding Your Dog Business: A Practical Guide to Business Success for Dog Professionals* and *The Business of Dog Walking: How to Make a Living Doing What You Love*. She lives with her husband surrounded by wildlife and dahlias on an Oregon coast hobby farm called, appropriately, River Dog Ranch.

Index

Dogwise.com is your source for quality books, ebooks, DVDs, training tools and treats.

We've been selling to the dog fancier for more than 25 years and we carefully screen our products for quality information, safety, durability and FUN! You'll find something for every level of dog enthusiast on our website www.dogwise.com or drop by our store in Wenatchee, Washington.

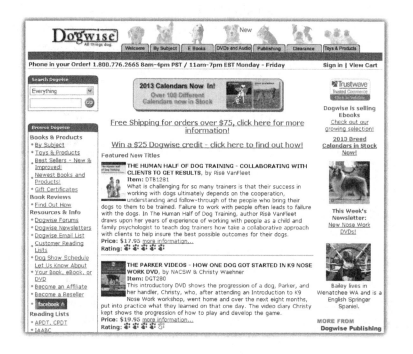

Made in the USA
Middletown, DE
25 October 2020